MW00574151

One Christ
MANY CREEDS

By Erik Rottmann

CONCORDIA PUBLISHING HOUSE · SAINT LOUIS

Copyright © 2008 Concordia Publishing House
3558 S. Jefferson Ave., St. Louis, MO 63118-3968
1-800-325-3040 • www.cph.org

All rights reserved. Unless specifically noted, no part of this publication may be reproduced, stored in a retrieval system, or transmitted, in any form or by any means, electronic, mechanical, photocopying, recording, or otherwise, without the prior written permission of Concordia Publishing House.

The purchaser of this publication is allowed to reproduce the marked portions contained herein for use with this curriculum. These resources may not be transferred or copied to another user.

Written by Erik Rottmann

Edited by Mark S. Sengele

Unless otherwise indicated, Scripture quotations are from The Holy Bible, English Standard Version®. Copyright © 2001 by Crossway Bibles, a publishing ministry of Good News Publishers, Wheaton, Illinois. Used by permission. All rights reserved.

Scripture quotations marked NIV are taken from the Holy Bible, New International Version®. NIV®. Copyright © 1973, 1978, 1984 by International Bible Society. Used by permission of Zondervan Publishing House. All rights reserved.

Selected quotes are from *What Luther Says: A Practical In-Home Anthology for the Active Christian.* Copyright © 1959 Concordia Publishing House. All rights reserved.

Quotations from the Small Catechism are taken from *Luther's Small Catechism with Explanation,* copyright © 1986, 1991 Concordia Publishing House, 2005 edition. All rights reserved.

The quotations from the Lutheran Confessions in this publication are from *Concordia: The Lutheran Confessions,* second edition, copyright © 2006 Concordia Publishing House. All rights reserved.

Quotations marked LW are from Luther's Works, American Edition: vol. 2 copyright © 1960; vol. 14 copyright © 1958; vol. 15 copyright © 1972; vol. 23 copyright © 1959; vol. 24 copyright © 1961; vol. 26 copyright © 1963; vol. 27 copyright © 1964; and vol. 30 copyright © 1967 by Concordia Publishing House; and vol. 40 copyright © 1958 by Fortress Press. Used by permission. All rights reserved.

Cover art: © iStockphto/Hazlan Abdul Hakim

Artwork on page 9 by Robert Hunt © Concordia Publishing House.

This publication may be available in braille, in large print, or on cassette tape for the visually impaired. Please allow 8 to 12 weeks for delivery. Write to Lutheran Blind Mission, 7550 Watson Rd., St. Louis, MO 63119-4409; call toll-free 1-888-215-2455; or visit the Web site: www.blindmission.org.

Manufactured in the United States of America

Your comments and suggestions concerning the material are appreciated. Please write to the Editor of Youth Materials, Concordia Publishing House, 3558 S. Jefferson Ave., St. Louis, MO 63118-3968.

1 2 3 4 5 6 7 8 9 10   17 16 15 14 13 12 11 10 09 08

Table of Contents

CONCORDIA UNIVERSITY LIBRARY
PORTLAND, OR 97211

About This Book

No one who is seriously Lutheran would ever maintain that only Lutherans are going to heaven, or that there are no Christians in other church bodies. On the other hand, no one who is seriously Lutheran would ever reject out of hand the notion that the differences between the various Christian church bodies are unimportant or superficial. There are important reasons—biblical reasons—why Lutherans are Lutheran and not Roman Catholic, Eastern Orthodox, Methodist, and so on.

On the surface, this Bible study is about the histories, concerns, and main teachings of various Christian church bodies. Beyond the surface, this Bible study is really about what Lutherans believe and why they believe it.

For the Instructor

How can you be *certain* beyond all doubt that your sins are *completely* forgiven by God? How can you be totally assured that when you die, you will go directly to heaven forever?

The certainty of your salvation comes only from God. You can only be certain of your forgiveness and salvation if God does 100 percent of the work and you do nothing. Stated another way, if you must personally contribute anything to your own salvation, you will never be certain that you have contributed enough, and therefore you will never be certain about your salvation.

This Bible study is all about certainty. This study was written to show you that the historic teachings of the Lutheran Church (drawn exclusively from the Scriptures) provide you with something that no other teachings from any other church body on earth can provide you: certainty. Assurance. Total confidence in Christ. The Lutheran Church is the only Christian church body in the world that teaches you to trust totally in Jesus and in no one else, not even yourself. Every other church body on earth teaches you to trust something else, at least in part, rather than to trust exclusively in Jesus.

As you prepare to teach *One Christ, Many Creeds*, you will note the following themes:

The Continual Return to God's Word

The main purpose of this study is to help you and your class emulate the Christians in Acts 17, studying the main doctrines of the major Christian church bodies and "examining the Scriptures . . . to see if these things were so" (Acts 17:11). This comparison of various church bodies will help you and your class listen more carefully to the Word of God, to "grow in the grace and knowledge of our Lord and Savior Jesus Christ" (2 Peter 3:18), and "to make a defense to anyone who asks you for a reason for the hope that is in you" (1 Peter 3:15).

A Deeper Understanding of the Lutheran Faith, Drawn Exclusively from the Word

You and your class will gain a greater understanding of what you believe by also understanding more clearly what you do *not* believe (and why you do not believe it). When the earliest Lutherans spoke about what they believed, they spoke also about what they did not believe, as a point of comparison.

Here's an example of what the earliest Lutherans stated that they believed: "Concerning Baptism, our churches teach that Baptism is necessary for salvation [Mark 16:16] and that God's grace is offered through Baptism [Titus 3:4–7]. They teach that children are to be baptized [Acts 2:38–39]. Being offered to God through Baptism, they are received into God's grace" (AC IX 1).

After stating what they believed, the early Lutherans also stated what they did not believe, so that no one might misunderstand their teachings: "Our churches condemn the Anabaptists, who reject the Baptism of children, and say that children are saved without Baptism" (AC IX 3).

Speaking to Other Christians

Many Lutherans have friends or family members who are members of other Christian church bodies. All Lutherans have daily opportunities to speak the faith to other Christians. A clear understanding of the distinctive teachings of the various church bodies will provide you and your class with important tools for profitable conversations.

Preparing to Teach

Procedures for conducting the class will vary according to the instructor's teaching style and experience. The following considerations may be helpful in preparing to teach:

- *Class Materials*: Each session has a Participant Page that may be reproduced for each student. Bibles will be necessary, and class participants may wish to have a pen or pencil for recording notes. According to your teaching style, you might also wish to use newsprint and markers, a whiteboard, or the like. The leader may also wish to reproduce copies of the Quick Comparison Charts to distribute in class.

- *Class Schedule:* Many Bible studies assume that a class session must be completed in forty-five minutes to an hour. This one-size-fits-all schedule might not work in every situation. Aside from your allotted class time, you might also want to consider other variables, such as the flow of conversation, class size, and the familiarity the participants have with one another. Do not feel compelled to complete a given session within a certain amount of time. If a particular session's materials have not yet been covered by the end of the allotted time, feel free to continue the same conversation and session materials during the next gathering of the class. On the other hand, if a session is completed before class time has expired, feel free to begin introducing the next session.

- *The Continual Return to God's Word*: As each respective church body is examined, everyone in the class will want to bear in mind the main purpose of this study, which is the study of God's Word, the Bible. Each class session will study several Bible passages, which the instructor should examine beforehand. An answer is provided for each study question, but these are necessarily short. Many of the answers are designed to stimulate group discussion. Opening and closing prayers likewise focus exclusively on the main point of the study.

• *Regular Review*: Over the course of this study, it might be helpful periodically to review with the class the introductory paragraph in the "Historical Context" section. Additionally, it might also be helpful during each class session to review the "General Introduction" of the respective unit before turning to each church body in that unit. This will help the participants to understand each church body in its larger historical context.

• *Lesson Focus*: Unlike its companion study, *One God, Many Gods* (a study of world religions), this study focuses primarily on Christian church bodies, which are also commonly referred to as "denominations." Many of the church bodies studied here teach many points in common with the teachings of the Lutheran Church, not the least of which are the Trinity and the two natures of Christ.

A Note from the Author

Some people might say that I have oversimplified the differences between Christian church bodies in this Bible study. I admit that these studies are very brief, and certainly they are no substitute for a more detailed examination of each church body. Oversimplification is necessary in a limited context such as the present study. That is why I have narrowed this study to the topic of certainty and how true Christian certainty may be found.

Due to space limitations, this study focuses mainly on the differences between the church bodies, making little mention of their commonalities. This focus is not intended to belittle or deride other Christians, but merely to highlight the weaknesses of the public teachings in other church bodies. This is done for two reasons: (a) that the class participants may understand and grow into their own faith more deeply, and (b) to impress upon the participants that differences in teachings truly matter, especially among Christians. As St. Paul said to Timothy, faithful teaching of the Scriptures is the nourishment of the faith. "If you put these things before the brothers, you will be a good servant of Christ Jesus, being trained [literally, "being nourished"] in the words of the faith and of the good doctrine that you have followed" (1 Timothy 4:6).

A group may be called Christian when it collectively believes and publicly confesses (a) that God is triune (that is, Father, Son, and Holy Spirit) and (b) that Christ has two natures (that is, Jesus Christ is both fully God and fully man). Stated another way, all the groups examined in this study are Christian because they agree to the teachings of the Athanasian Creed, even if some of them generally do not make use of this creed in their worship. There is but one exception to this rule: a branch of the Pentecostals called "Oneness Pentecostals" has recently begun denying the Trinity in its public teaching. According to the Athanasian Creed, this branch of the Pentecostals no longer is rightly called Christian (even though this group still calls itself Christian). However, because a large portion of the Pentecostals have not yet denied the Trinity, the Pentecostals as a whole are examined here as a Christian church body.

Unit I
The Ancient Church Bodies

Lutherans (Historic)
Roman Catholicism
Eastern Orthodoxy

General Introduction

As Christianity spread throughout the ancient world, important ecclesiastical centers were founded in major cities. These centers can be divided into two groups: the Latin Church in the West (headed by the Bishop of Rome, the pope) and the Greek Churches in the East (with bishops in Constantinople, Jerusalem, Alexandria, and Antioch). Tensions grew between the East and the West over time, leading to the Great Schism of 1054. Some of these tensions were over matters of theology. At their root, however, was a quest for power. The Bishop of Rome wanted to claim supremacy over the Eastern bishops.

One of the main reasons for the Great Schism was disagreement over whether the words "and the Son" should be used in the Nicene Creed. (The Holy Spirit "proceeds from the Father and the Son.") While the Latin Church insisted that these words represented good and faithful theology that should be added to the creed, the Greek Churches refused. The phrase was not in the original wording of the creed, argued the Greeks, and thus it does not belong there. Tradition is very important for the Greek Churches, and they did not want to change their tradition by including the new phrase in the Nicene Creed.

The Great Schism led to the development of the two largest church bodies in the world, which are today known as the Roman Catholic Church and the Eastern Orthodox Church.

About five hundred years after the Great Schism, the Lutheran Church likewise formed. In a manner similar to the Eastern Churches, the Lutheran Church came about as the result of a dispute with Rome. However, tradition was not the main concern for the Lutherans. The Lutherans were concerned about faithfulness to the Bible. They believed that the Roman Church had moved away from the clear teachings of the Bible and needed to move back.

It may seem strange to include the Lutheran Church in the unit called "The Ancient Church Bodies." As shown by the following quotation, the Lutheran Church is included here because the earliest Lutherans confessed that they were not teaching something new. Rather, the earliest Lutherans were holding and teaching the doctrines of the Scriptures, as had many Christians before them.

There is nothing [in our teaching] that varies from the Scriptures, or from the Church universal, or from the Church of Rome. . . . Our churches do not dissent from any article of the faith held by the Church catholic. They only omit some of the newer abuses. (AC XXI 1)

1

Lutherans (Historic)

Lesson Focus

While it is impossible to review all the historic teachings of the Lutheran Church, those teachings are examined in this session that will provide a sturdy foundation for comparing the teachings of the other Christian church bodies.

Historical Context

Many people identify October 31, 1517, as the beginning of the Lutheran Reformation. This is the date on which Martin Luther nailed his famous Ninety-five Theses to the chapel door in Wittenberg. However, the Ninety-five Theses publicly announced something that already had been happening in private for several years—Luther had been studying God's Word, the Bible. Truly, the Lutheran Reformation owes its beginning not so much to the Ninety-five Theses, but to the miraculous work that God exerted by means of His powerful Word. God's Word first worked on Luther through Luther's careful study of the Scriptures. Then the Word of God worked through Luther as Luther proclaimed the Word by means of his preaching, teaching, and writing.

The earliest Lutherans (and the "historic" Lutherans of today) understood that eternal life and salvation come only though God's powerful Word. To move away from the Word is to move away from eternal life! This is why the earliest Lutherans used such words as *adversaries, false teachers*, and even *heretics* to describe those who moved away from the Word. The Lutherans did not use these terms to be malicious or to suggest that only Lutherans would go to heaven. The earliest Lutherans used such terms to warn other Christians so that they might not be led away from God's Word and the eternal life it brings. This is why the Lutherans warned in the Apology to the Augsburg Confession, "The adversaries corrupt very many [Bible] passages, because they bring to them their own opinions and do not derive the meaning from the passages themselves" (Ap V [III] 103).

Distribute copies of Participant Page 1 and the appropriate Quick Comparison Chart if desired. Begin by reviewing the message from Martin Luther and then open with the responsive prayer.

A Message from Martin Luther

Where eternal life and salvation are concerned, St. Peter and all godly men dismiss all other doctrines and know of none but that of this one Man Christ, of whom St. Peter declares: "You have the words of eternal life." Those words will satisfy me. This is beautifully spoken. He [Peter] will . . . cling to His [Christ's] words. And to them we, too, will adhere; for these words impart eternal life. St. Peter hits the nail on the head. (LW 23:194)

Opening Prayer

L: Jesus said, "Do you want to go away as well?"

P: Peter's response is also ours: "Lord, to whom shall we go? You have the words of eternal life." (John 6:68)

L: Blessed are those who hear the Word of God and keep it.

P: **Lord, keep us steadfast in Your Word!**

L: Open our eyes, O Lord, that we may behold wondrous things out of Your Word.

P: **Amen!**

Core Truths

Have participants work through these sections on their own using the Participant Page and their Bibles. As they complete each section, review and discuss together.

The central idea in the Lutheran confession of the Christian faith is that Jesus Christ has done absolutely everything for you and for your salvation. You are required to add nothing in order to be saved. If any teaching in the Church does not credit Christ with having done all things for your salvation, this teaching will not fail to "hide Christ's glory and benefits, and rob devout consciences of the consolation offered in Christ" (Ap IV [II] 3). Think about your relationship to Christ in mathematical terms. If Christ has done 100 percent of the work for your salvation, what percentage must you contribute? Zero! On the other hand, if someone teaches that you must personally contribute something, perhaps only 1 or 2 percent, this means that Christ has accomplished only 99 or 98 percent of your redemption. "What is this other than to deny Christ the honor of Mediator and Atoning Sacrifice?" (Ap V [III] 92).

What do the following verses have to say about Christ's work of salvation for you?

John 3:16–17—Salvation not only begins with God, but it is carried out for the whole world. Stated another way, Christ died for every sin committed by every person in the history and the future of the world. There is no one whose sins were not included in Christ's death and resurrection.

1 John 2:2—Christ is the "propitiation for our sins," that is, the full payment, satisfaction, appeasement, and atonement for our sins.

What do the following verses have to say about our ability to make a contribution to our own salvation apart from the indwelling of Christ?

Acts 5:31; 11:18—Repentance is not something we can bring about by our own strength, but something God gives to both the Jew and the Gentile alike.

Romans 8:7—Apart from God's miracle-producing Word, our minds remain hostile to Him. That is to say, sin has placed our minds into such bondage that apart from God's gifts of His Word and faith, we have no alternative but to hate God.

Ephesians 2:1—Apart from Christ, we are "dead in the trespasses and sins." Dead men can do nothing, including making contributions or commitments to their own salvation!

Discuss: *If the preceding passages are true (and we believe they are), how is it possible for anyone even to believe in Jesus? Use Romans 10:17; Ephesians 2:8–9; and John 11:38–44 for guidance in your discussion.* (We believe, but only because God first makes us able to believe by giving us His gift of faith. The miracle of raising Lazarus from the dead provides a good analogy for how God saves us. Like Lazarus, we were dead. By the miraculous power of His Word, Christ called to us, at the same time giving us both the gift of salvation and the ability to believe.)

Only the Word

Because Christ's work for your salvation was fully completed for you many centuries ago, we have no reliable source of the knowledge of salvation except for God's Word, the Bible. In the Bible, we not only have an authoritative, divinely inspired source of the knowledge of salvation, but we also have the power of the divine Word, which makes us able to believe and to be saved!

What do the following Bible verses have to say about the inspiration and authority of the Word?

John 20:31—The Scriptures were written to you so that you may believe "Jesus is the Christ, the Son of God, and that by believing you may have life in His name."

2 Timothy 3:16–17—The Scriptures are "God-breathed" (NIV), containing the same miraculous power of life that God also breathed into Adam (compare Genesis 2:7). Through His Scriptures, God likewise breathes eternal life into you.

2 Peter 1:21—The Scriptures are not man-made documents, but "men spoke from God as they were carried along by the Holy Spirit."

What do the following verses say about the power of the Word?

Isaiah 55:10–11—God's powerful Word accomplishes what He desires.

Jeremiah 1:12—God carefully watches over His Word "to perform it." That is to say, the Word is not mere information, but divine power that God exerts in the world.

Jeremiah 23:29—God's Word is compared to a rock-smashing hammer and a burning fire.

1 Thessalonians 2:13—Just as yeast works in a lump of dough, raising it up, so also "the word of God . . . is at work in you believers."

Discuss: *In what way does this teaching of both the inspiration and the power of the Word provide you with comfort and certainty in your salvation?* (Answers may vary. The inspiration of the Word gives us confidence that the words in the Bible are truly from God, and not something we have dreamed up for ourselves. The power of the Word offers great comfort and certainty because it promises to give us everything, including the power to believe.)

Certain Faith

The certainty of your salvation rests on the fact that you contribute nothing, but that God has done all things for you, including delivering salvation to you. It is for your certainty that God uses His Word to deliver to you not only the Good News about Jesus, but also the miraculous ability to believe this Good News. (See the preceding discussion question.) But the miraculous power of God's Word comes to you in more ways than one! While you can read the Bible and hear it read, God has also placed the power of His Word in the Sacraments of Baptism and Holy Communion for you!

In what way do the following verses show you how Baptism is God's act for you, delivering forgiveness to you?

John 3:3—"Born again" could equally be translated "born from above," which shows that the birth of Baptism is truly from God.

Titus 3:5–7—Baptism is a washing that the Holy Spirit performs for us.

1 Peter 3:21—"Baptism . . . now saves you." That is to say, Baptism does something for you, through the powerful Word of God. If Baptism were truly something you do for God, this verse would need to be worded differently, such as "Baptism now shows your commitment."

What are the key words in Matthew 26:26–28 that show how Holy Communion is also God's act for you, delivering forgiveness to you? (The key words are "for you." Holy Communion is God's miraculous act in which He gives you the benefits of Christ's death on the cross.)

Discuss: *When you understand clearly that the Word, Baptism, and Holy Communion are God's ways of delivering salvation to you, what perspective does this give you on the Third Commandment?* (Answers may vary. The main point is not what you do for God in worship, but what God does for you in worship. When Christians gather, God speaks His life-giving, forgiving Word to them. God nourishes them. God brings to their memory His adoptive act of baptizing them.)

Closing Prayer

Close with the following prayer.

Almighty God, our heavenly Father, because of Your tender love toward us sinners You have given Your Son that, believing in Him, we might have everlasting life. Continue to grant us Your Holy Spirit that we may remain steadfast in this faith to the end and finally come to life everlasting; through Jesus Christ, our Lord. Amen. (*LSB*, p. 311)

1 Lutherans (Historic)

A Message from Martin Luther

Where eternal life and salvation are concerned, St. Peter and all godly men dismiss all other doctrines and know of none but that of this one Man Christ, of whom St. Peter declares: "You have the words of eternal life." Those words will satisfy me. This is beautifully spoken. He [Peter] will . . . cling to His [Christ's] words. And to them we, too, will adhere; for these words impart eternal life. St. Peter hits the nail on the head. (LW 23:194)

Opening Prayer

L: Jesus said, "Do you want to go away as well?"

P: Peter's response is also ours: "Lord, to whom shall we go? You have the words of eternal life." (John 6:68)

L: Blessed are those who hear the Word of God and keep it.

P: Lord, keep us steadfast in Your Word!

L: Open our eyes, O Lord, that we may behold wondrous things out of Your Word.

P: Amen!

Core Truths

What do the following verses have to say about Christ's work of salvation for you?

John 3:16–17

1 John 2:2

What do the following verses have to say about our ability to make a contribution to our own salvation apart from the indwelling of Christ?

Acts 5:31; 11:18

Romans 8:7

Ephesians 2:1

If the preceding passages are true (and we believe they are), how is it possible for anyone even to believe in Jesus? Use **Romans 10:17**; **Ephesians 2:8–9**; and **John 11:38–44** for guidance in your discussion.

Only the Word

What do the following Bible verses have to say about the inspiration and authority of the Word?

John 20:31

2 Timothy 3:16–17

2 Peter 1:21

What do the following verses say about the power of the Word?

Isaiah 55:10–11

Jeremiah 1:12

Jeremiah 23:29

1 Thessalonians 2:13

In what way does this teaching of both the inspiration and the power of the Word provide you with comfort and certainty in your salvation?

Certain Faith

In what way do the following verses show you how Baptism is God's act for you, delivering forgiveness to you?

John 3:3

Titus 3:5–7

1 Peter 3:21

What are the key words in **Matthew 26:26–28** that show how Holy Communion is also God's act for you, delivering forgiveness to you?

When you understand clearly that the Word, Baptism, and Holy Communion are God's ways of delivering salvation to you, what perspective does this give you on the Third Commandment, "Remember the Sabbath day, to keep it holy" (**Exodus 20:8**)?

Participant Page 1 *One Christ, Many Creeds* copyright © 2008 Concordia Publishing House. Scripture: ESV* Luther's Works, American Edition: vol. 23 copyright © 1959 Concordia Publishing House. All rights reserved. Reproduced by permission.

2

Roman Catholicism

Lesson Focus

In Christ, we have a sure salvation; eternal life with Him is certain. In this session, we focus on the particular teachings of the Roman Catholic Church—especially the doctrine of the papacy—that illustrate how this church body's teachings are geared toward promoting uncertainty.

Historical Context

One of the core teachings of the Roman Catholic Church is the authority of the Roman bishop, also known as the pope. (His office is referred to as the "papacy.") Rome's claim to papal authority dates back to the early centuries of Church history, predating both the Lutheran Reformation and the Great Schism. In fact, the papacy claims that its authority and supremacy can be traced all the way to Saints Peter and Paul.

Because papal authority is so important to Rome, the Word of God is required to take a backseat. Stated another way, the Bible is not the final source and authority of Roman Catholic teachings. Rather, the pope's authoritative explanation of the Bible is the source. When the pope speaks authoritatively, either in keeping with Scripture or in going beyond what is written in the Scriptures, he is said to be speaking *ex cathedra*, or "out of his seat/ office." The papacy claims that God speaks to the pope apart from the Scriptures, and the pope then speaks to the Church and the world.

Ultimately, this insistence on papal authority is what led to the Lutheran Reformation. Luther originally voiced his scriptural protests against certain teachings and practices because he believed that if the pope only knew what falsehoods were being promoted, these abuses would soon be ended. Later, Luther realized that the papacy not only promoted these nonbiblical teachings and practices, but was also profiting from them!

Distribute copies of Participant Page 2 and, if desired, the appropriate Quick Comparison Chart. Begin by reviewing the message from Martin Luther and then open with the responsive prayer.

A Message from Martin Luther

"The papacy is just as useful to the church as the fifth wheel on a wagon. It is, in fact, entirely harmful" (*What Luther Says* § 3194).

Opening Prayer

L: There is one mediator between God and men, the man Christ Jesus,

P: Who gave Himself as a ransom for all.
(1 Timothy 2:5–6)

L: Let us then with confidence draw near to the throne of grace,

P: That we may receive mercy and find grace to help in time of need. (Hebrews 4:16)

L: Open our eyes, O Lord, that we may behold wondrous things out of Your Word.

P: Amen!

The Word

Direct participants back to the Participant Page and ask them to work through this section. Roman Catholicism believes in the Bible, but the Bible as it must be interpreted according to the pope's authority. According to the *Catechism of the Catholic Church*:

> "*Sacred Scripture* is the speech of God as it is put down in writing under the breath of the Holy Spirit." "And [Holy] *Tradition* transmits in its entirety the Word of God which has been entrusted to the apostles by Christ the Lord and the Holy Spirit. It transmits it to the successors of the apostles so that, enlightened by the Spirit of truth, they may faithfully preserve, expound, and spread it abroad by their preaching. As a result the Church, to whom the transmission and interpretation of Revelation is entrusted, "does not derive her certainty about all revealed truths from the holy Scriptures alone. Both Scripture and Tradition must be accepted and honored with equal sentiments of devotion and reverence" (*Catechism of the Catholic Church*, § 81–82, http://www.vatican.va/archive).

Stated another way, the pope, informed by Scripture and church tradition, can tell you what to believe. For many years, Catholic families felt no need for a Bible. They only needed to listen to the priest, who spoke on behalf of the pope. (This belief has begun to change.)

The papacy builds on the assumption that the Bible is a dark book, and that special insight is needed to understand it. What do the following Bible passages have to say about God's Word, the Bible?

Psalm 119:105—While the Bible may indeed have passages that are difficult to understand, on the whole it is a clear "lamp to my feet and a light to my path."

2 Peter 1:16–19—Peter saw the amazing and awe-inspiring transfiguration of our Lord on the mountaintop, but he declares that not even the transfiguration is as sure and certain as "the prophetic word," which declares Christ to you. The Bible is not a series of "cleverly devised myths" but a sure and certain revelation that shines brightly like "a lamp shining in a dark place."

Discuss: *Do the preceding Bible passages mean that people should not have a pastor or shepherd to guide them? What is the benefit of the Office of the Ministry if everyone can read the Bible for himself or herself? Compare Romans 10:14–17; 1 Corinthians 4:1–4; and Ephesians 4:11–14 in guiding your answer.* (Answers will vary. God gave pastors as gifts to the Church, as Ephesians 4:11–14 states. Pastors are not given so that the people can have someone lord it over them, but so that God's people can hear His Word proclaimed and receive His Sacraments for the benefit of their souls [Luke 22:25–26; 1 Corinthians 4:1–4; 2 Timothy 4:1–5]. God sends pastors to His Church, not to abuse the Scriptures by claiming authority over it, but to see that the Scriptures are faithfully proclaimed and taught to the people.)

What is Jesus speaking about in Matthew 23:9? (When Jesus says "Call no man your father on earth," He is not saying that no one should have authority over you! Not only would such an understanding of this verse contradict other passages of the Bible [Romans 13:1; Hebrews 13:7], but this understanding would also make it a sin for a little child to call his daddy "father." Jesus is saying that "you only have one Father, who is in heaven." All other authorities—including the earthly office of father, or daddy—are given by God. These authorities are not given to you so that they may lord it over you, but so that they may serve your physical and spiritual needs.)

Confession

In Roman Catholicism, private confession is a required act in which you must enumerate every sin so that you may do penance, or pay satisfactions, for your offenses. The satisfactions required of you might include praying the rosary a certain number of times, paying compensation for wrongs committed, making an offering, performing works of service, and so on. According to the *Catechism of the Catholic Church*:

> Absolution [that is, the word of forgiveness] takes away sin, but it does not remedy all the disorders sin has caused. Raised up from sin, the sin-

ner must still recover his full spiritual health by doing something more to make amends for the sin: he must "make satisfaction for" or "expiate" his sins. This satisfaction is also called "penance" (*Catechism of the Catholic Church*, § 1459, http://www.vatican.va/archive).

What do the following Bible verses say about our ability to know, much less confess, every one of our sins?

Psalm 19:12—David, like all other people, cannot list all his sins because he knows he has hidden faults that he cannot comprehend, much less enumerate.

Psalm 40:12—"My iniquities . . . are more than the hairs of my head."

Matthew 6:12—When we pray in the Lord's Prayer "Forgive us our debts [trespasses]," we are pleading guilty to all sins, even those of which we might not be aware.

Romans 8:26—The Spirit helps us in our weakness because we are unable fully to discern what we need to pray.

Discuss: *What do you think of the Roman teaching that you must "make amends" for the sins you commit against others? Is there anything about this teaching that is good and beneficial? What are the dangers of this teaching? Use Luke 19:1–10; Romans 13:1–7; and 1 John 2:2 for guidance in your discussion.* (Answers will vary. If you wrong your neighbor in some way, such as stealing from him or her, it is a good and loving thing to restore what you have stolen. This act not only returns the lost item to its rightful owner, but you also show by your actions that you are truly sorry for your sins. Someone who commits a crime is fully forgiven by Christ, but he or she may still owe a civil penalty to the government. However, to speak about such things as "expiation" is to lead people to believe that these acts will also benefit them before God. Contrary to this thinking, Christ alone is the expiation for sins.)

Discuss: *In what way is the Lutheran practice of confession and absolution different from the Roman practice of confession and satisfaction?* (Answers will vary. It might be helpful to read Luther's Small Catechism on this point:

Confession has two parts. First, that we confess our sins, and second, that we receive absolution, that is, forgiveness, from the pastor as from God Himself, not doubting, but firmly believing that by it our sins are forgiven before God in heaven [p. 26].)

Purgatory

Over the centuries, the papacy has introduced a huge burden of uncertainty into the Roman Catholic Church through its distribution (and sale) of indulgences. Back in the days of the Reformation, a person could buy a piece of paper from the papacy that earned forgiveness of sins or release from purgatory. (The very teaching of purgatory itself is not from the Bible.) Some people say that indulgences are no longer used in the Roman Catholic Church today, yet the pope issued an indulgence to celebrate the Year of Jubilee in 2000. The basic teachings of the Roman Catholic Church have not substantially changed since Martin Luther was alive.

Discuss: *In what way does Rome's false teaching of purgatory take away your certainty and replace it with fear?* (Answers will vary. Purgatory waits for those who do not sufficiently expiate or "make amends" for their sin. When a person dies, he or she goes to purgatory to suffer for a while. This teaching replaces the comforts of forgiveness with the fear of punishment, robbing you of the certainty both of God's mercy and your salvation.)

Closing Prayer

Almighty and everlasting God, through Your Son You have promised us forgiveness of sins and everlasting life. Govern our hearts by Your Holy Spirit that in our daily need, and especially in all time of temptation, we may seek Your help and, by a true and lively faith in Your Word, obtain all that You have promised; through the same Jesus Christ, our Lord. Amen. (*LSB*, p. 312)

2 Roman Catholicism

A Message from Martin Luther

The papacy is just as useful to the church as the fifth wheel on a wagon. It is, in fact, entirely harmful. (*What Luther Says* § 3194)

Opening Prayer

L: There is one mediator between God and men, the man Christ Jesus,

P: Who gave Himself as a ransom for all. (1 Peter 2:5–6)

L: Let us then with confidence draw near to the throne of grace,

P: That we may receive mercy and find grace to help in time of need. (Hebrews 4:16)

L: Open our eyes, O Lord, that we may behold wondrous things out of Your Word.

P: Amen!

The Word

The papacy builds on the assumption that the Bible is a dark book, and that special insight is needed to understand it. What do the following Bible passages have to say about God's Word, the Bible?

Psalm 119:105

_____

2 Peter 1:16–19

_____

Do the preceding Bible passages mean that people should not have a pastor or shepherd to guide them? What is the benefit of the Office of the Ministry if everyone can read the Bible for himself or herself? Compare **Romans 10:14–17**; **1 Corinthians 4:1–4**; and **Ephesians 4:11–14** in guiding your answer.

_____

_____

What is Jesus speaking about in **Matthew 23:9**?

_____

_____

_____

Confession

What do the following Bible verses say about our ability to know, much less confess, every one of our sins?

Psalm 19:12

_____

_____

Psalm 40:12

_____

_____

Matthew 6:12

_____

_____

Romans 8:26

_____

_____

What do you think of the Roman teaching that you must "make amends" for the sins you commit against others? Is there anything about this teaching that is good and beneficial? What are the dangers of this teaching? Use **Luke 19:1–10**; **Romans 13:1–7**; and **1 John 2:2** for guidance in your discussion.

_____

_____

In what way is the Lutheran practice of confession and absolution different from the Roman practice of confession and satisfaction?

_____

_____

_____

Purgatory

In what way does Rome's false teaching of purgatory take away your certainty and replace it with fear?

_____

_____

_____

Participant Page 2 *One Christ, Many Creeds* copyright © 2008 Concordia Publishing House. Scripture: ESV® *What Luther Says: A Practical In-Home Anthology for the Active Christian* copyright © 1959 Concordia Publishing House. All rights reserved. Reproduced by permission.

3

Eastern Orthodoxy

Lesson Focus

In Christ, we have a sure salvation; eternal life with Him is certain. In this session, we focus primarily on the denial of original sin, a doctrine of the Eastern Orthodox Churches that teaches you to look inside yourself for your certainty, rather than exclusively toward Christ.

Historical Context

There are various Eastern Orthodox Churches, organized by nationality (Greek, Russian, Bulgarian, Romanian, and so on), including the Orthodox Church in America. While each has its own bishop, each Eastern Orthodox Church also recognizes the honorary authority of the Patriarch of Constantinople. The Eastern Orthodox Churches have a common theology, which has ancient roots (see the General Introduction to the Ancient Church Bodies). This common theology includes a high view of liturgical worship, the Ecumenical Creeds, and a strong aversion to the Roman papacy, resulting from the Great Schism.

Prior to the Great Schism, the Eastern Churches also produced some of the most influential theologians in Christian history, whose works are studied in many Christian church bodies even today. Many Christians feel a sense of attraction to Eastern Orthodoxy. The attraction comes not only from these influential theologians or from the high view of the liturgy, but also from the beautiful art of Eastern Orthodoxy, known as iconography.

Those who feel attracted by the beauty of Eastern Orthodoxy must be careful! Some teachings held by this group of churches not only depart from God's Word, the Bible, but also take away from the honor and glory that are due to Christ alone. Chief among the Eastern Orthodox teachings that rob Christ are the denial of the Bible's teaching concerning original sin. This denial of original sin is related to Eastern Orthodoxy's belief that in order to be justified, both faith and works are necessary.

Distribute copies of Participant Page 3 and begin by reviewing the message from the Lutheran Confessions; then open with the responsive prayer. If desired, you may also distribute copies of the appropriate Quick Comparison Chart at this time.

A Message from the Lutheran Confessions

Our churches teach that since the fall of Adam [Romans 5:12], all who are naturally born are born with sin [Psalm 51:5], that is, without the fear of God, without trust in God, and with the inclination to sin, called concupiscence. Concupiscence is a disease and original vice that is truly sin. It damns and brings eternal death on those who are not born anew through Baptism and the Holy Spirit [John 3:5].
(AC II 1)

Opening Prayer

L: Behold, I was brought forth in iniquity, and in sin did my mother conceive me. (Psalm 51:5)

P: None is righteous, no, not one. (Romans 3:10)

L: Grace abounded all the more, so that, as sin reigned in death,

P: Grace also might reign through righteousness leading to eternal life through Jesus Christ our Lord. (Romans 5:20–21)

L: Open our eyes, O Lord, that we may behold wondrous things out of Your Word.

P: Amen!

Original Sin

Direct participants to this section and work through it together. As stated in the Historical Context section, the Orthodox Churches reject the concept of original sin. They teach that deep within man, there is some part that remains unspoiled by sin. The Lutheran Church teaches that by nature, we have concupiscence. "This means people not only lack fear and trust in God, but also do not even have the power or gifts to produce fear and trust in God" (Ap II 3).

Discuss: *If there is still a portion of you that has retained a part—even a small part—of God's grace, how much of you needs to be redeemed by Jesus? Asked another way, what does the Orthodox denial of original sin say about Christ's work on the cross?* (Answers may vary. If there is a small part of you that does not need redemption and forgiveness because it was not destroyed in the fall, then that same small part of you does not need Jesus. Stated another way, Christ only died and rose for part of you, not the whole you from head to toe.)

What do the following passages from the Bible have to say about Christ and His work for you?

Isaiah 48:11—"My glory I will not give to another." God does not want to share any of His redeeming work with you, which is what happens if there is still some part of you that He does not need to redeem.

Hebrews 12:2—Jesus is the "author and perfecter of our faith" (NIV).

Revelation 22:13—Jesus is the beginning and the end. That is to say, He has accomplished all things for us and for our salvation.

According to Ephesians 2:1–5, does the problem of sin consist merely of a darkening of the mind and an impairment of the will, or does the problem run a bit deeper? (The problem of sin is more than a darkening of the mind or an impairment of the will. We were dead in sin, and dead people make no contribution to their own salvation.)

In what way do Romans 5:10 and Romans 8:7 add to the picture of original sin? (We are not merely dead; the fall into sin made us "enemies" and "hostile to God" rather than friendly, responsive, and helpful toward Him.)

Discuss: *In what way might the Orthodox denial of original sin tempt you to trust in something other than Christ alone for your salvation?* (Answers may vary. If there is a small part of you that was not ruined by the fall into sin, then there is a small part of you that you can trust in, rather than trusting in Christ alone.)

Our Source

Continue with this section, having participants work together in pairs or small groups. The Orthodox Churches also teach that while humankind may not deserve salvation, we must certainly work for it, since "faith by itself, if it does not have works, is dead" (James 2:17). They confuse the sanctified behavior of a believer with the requirement for justification.

In what way do the following Bible verses seem to support the Orthodox idea that a person must cooperate with God in working for his or her salvation?

1 Corinthians 3:9—Paul describes himself and the other apostles as God's "fellow workers," working along with Him.

Philippians 2:12—"Work out your own salvation with fear and trembling."

James 2:14–20—"Faith without works is dead."

According to the following verses, what is the source of our strength or ability to "work out our salvation" and participate in good works?

Galatians 2:20—"It is no longer I who live, but Christ who lives in me."

Philippians 2:13—Remember while you are working out your salvation "with fear and trembling" (v. 12) that it is actually "God who works in you, both to will and to work for His good pleasure." We cooperate or work together with God only when God has powerfully begun to reestablish His will in us through His miraculous gift of faith.

1 Thessalonians 2:13—The power of sanctification is not your inborn ability, but the Word that "is at work in you who believe" (NIV).

In what way do the preceding Bible verses help shape your understanding of Matthew 25:31–46? For additional help, read Hebrews 11:6. (The sheep and the goats are undoubtedly judged on the basis of their works, whether or not they have cared for their neighbor as the Christian faith requires. However, the preceding verses, along with many others, show that "without faith it is impossible to please [God].")

Discuss: *Which offers you more comfort and certainty of salvation: the Orthodox idea that you must contribute something from within yourself, or the Bible's teaching that God Himself lives and works in you and through you?* (Answers may vary. If Christ has completely and totally done all things for your salvation, you can trust without doubt that you shall be saved. If you personally have to become involved, uncertainty inevitably enters. How can you ever be sure you have been involved enough?)

Closing Prayer

Almighty and everlasting God, You would have all to be saved and to come to the knowledge of the truth. By Your almighty power and unsearchable wisdom break and hinder all the counsels of those who hate Your Word and who, by corrupt teaching, would destroy it. Enlighten them with the knowledge of Your glory that they may know the riches of Your heavenly grace and, in peace and righteousness, serve You, the only true God; through Jesus Christ, our Lord. Amen. (*LSB*, p. 305).

3 Eastern Orthodoxy

A Message from the Lutheran Confessions

Our churches teach that since the fall of Adam [Romans 5:12], all who are naturally born are born with sin [Psalm 51:5], that is, without the fear of God, without trust in God, and with the inclination to sin, called concupiscence. Concupiscence is a disease and original vice that is truly sin. It damns and brings eternal death on those who are not born anew through Baptism and the Holy Spirit [John 3:5]. (AC II 1)

Opening Prayer

L: Behold, I was brought forth in iniquity, and in sin did my mother conceive me. (Psalm 51:5)

P: **None is righteous, no, not one.** (Romans 3:10)

L: Grace abounded all the more, so that, as sin reigned in death,

P: **Grace also might reign through righteousness leading to eternal life through Jesus Christ our Lord.** (Romans 5:20–21)

L: Open our eyes, O Lord, that we may behold wondrous things out of Your Word.

P: **Amen!**

Original Sin

If there is still a portion of you that has retained a part—even a small part—of God's grace, how much of you needs to be redeemed by Jesus? Asked another way, what does the Orthodox denial of original sin say about Christ's work on the cross?

_____

What do the following passages from the Bible have to say about Christ and His work for you?

Isaiah 48:11

Hebrews 12:2

Revelation 22:13

According to **Ephesians 2:1–5**, does the problem of sin consist merely of a darkening of the mind and an impairment of the will, or does the problem run a bit deeper?

_____

In what way do **Romans 5:10** and **Romans 8:7** add to the picture of original sin?

_____

In what way might the Orthodox denial of original sin tempt you to trust in something other than Christ alone for your salvation?

_____

Our Source

In what way do the following Bible verses seem to support the Orthodox idea that a person must cooperate with God in working for his or her salvation?

1 Corinthians 3:9

Philippians 2:12

James 2:14–20

According to the following verses, what is the source of our strength or ability to "work out our salvation" and participate in good works?

Galatians 2:20

Philippians 2:13

1 Thessalonians 2:13

In what way do the preceding Bible verses help shape your understanding of **Matthew 25:31–46**? For additional help, read **Hebrews 11:6**.

_____

Which offers you more comfort and certainty of salvation: the Orthodox idea that you must contribute something from within yourself, or the Bible's teaching that God Himself lives and works in you and through you?

_____

Participant Page 3 *One Christ, Many Creeds* copyright © 2008 Concordia Publishing House. Scripture: ESV® *Concordia: The Lutheran Confessions*, second edition, copyright © 2006 Concordia Publishing House. All rights reserved. Reproduced by permission.

Unit II
Calvinist Church Bodies

Presbyterians
Christian Reformed
Addendum: Anglicans/Episcopalians

General Introduction

Martin Luther (1483–1546) sought to correct the abuses in the Church of Rome by means of clear and simple teaching from the Word of God. One of Luther's contemporaries, John Calvin (1509–1564), had different desires. Calvin was a theologian and church leader who sought a complete break with Rome.

Calvin was born in France, but his break from Rome forced him to move to Switzerland, where he could live free from persecution. In Switzerland, Calvin wrote his extremely influential *Institutes of the Christian Religion.* With the help of friends, Calvin also established a government in Geneva that he believed was based on the example of the Old Testament. Under Calvin's leadership, governmental power was placed in the hands of four classes of men: pastors, doctors, elders, and deacons. These men had the authority to oversee moral behavior and to inflict harsh punishments on those who indulged in such fleshly pleasures as dancing and playing games. Opponents of Calvin's regime were tortured and executed, and he eventually enjoyed unopposed leadership of Geneva during the final decade of his life.

The key theological points of Calvin's *Institutes* are easily summarized with the acronym **TULIP**:

Total depravity of man (We can do nothing good, not even respond to God's call.)

Unconditional election (God saves people by His mercy alone.)

Limited atonement (Jesus died for some, but not for all.)

Irresistible grace (If you are chosen for salvation, there is no way you can avoid it.)

Perseverance of the saints (Once you are saved, you are always saved.)

Many church bodies trace at least a portion of their history to Calvin's teachings. However, the more prominent Calvinist bodies today are the Presbyterians and the Christian Reformed. While each of these bodies has a unique history, they are theologically similar because of their common roots.

The Anglican/Episcopalian Church is not technically a Calvinist church body. It is included in this unit because it was the seedbed out of which arose a strong Calvinist movement called Puritanism. The Pilgrims who came to America on the Mayflower in 1620 were Puritans.

4

Presbyterians

Lesson Focus

In Christ, we have a sure salvation; eternal life with Him is certain. In this session, we focus primarily on the idea of limited atonement, the first element of John Calvin's theology that creates uncertainty. This element of Calvin's theology is essential to Calvin's basic theological thought: that God is sovereign and can do anything He wishes to do.

Historical Context

John Calvin did not directly establish the Presbyterian church bodies. However, these bodies were built on the foundation of his teachings, most especially Calvin's emphasis on the absolute sovereignty of God. Several strands of Presbyterianism took root in various countries, including France (the Huguenots), Holland (the Dutch Reformed), and Scotland.

The term *Presbyterian* has to do with the form of governance in which a small group leads the entire church body, as happened in Geneva under Calvin's rule. (See the General Introduction to the Calvinist Church Bodies.)

Scottish Presbyterians trace their historical roots to the work and teachings of John Knox (1505–1572), who became a leader in establishing Calvinism in Scotland after he was driven from England during the reign of Queen Mary, a staunch Roman Catholic. From Scotland, Presbyterianism eventually spread back to England, and then beyond England to the British colonies in America.

There are various Presbyterian church bodies in the United States today, some of which remain very close to historic Calvinism with its "TULIP" theology and its strong emphasis on authority and inspiration of the Scriptures. Other Presbyterian bodies might be characterized as more liberal. This means that these bodies no longer place a major emphasis on the Scriptures as the inspired Word of God. This,

in turn, has led to the practice of women's ordination; the teaching that homosexuality is not so much a sin as an alternative lifestyle; and so on. (These worldly influences will be discussed further in Unit 5, Late Arrivals).

Distribute copies of Participant Page 4 and the Quick Comparison Chart for this lesson. Begin by reviewing the Message from Martin Luther, and then open with the responsive prayer.

A Message from Martin Luther

Especially practice this pronoun "our" in such a way that this syllable, once believed, may swallow up and absorb all your sins, that is, that you may be certain that Christ has taken away not only the sins of some men but your sins and those of the whole world. . . . That is, believe that Christ was given not only for the sins of others but also for yours. Hold to this firmly, and do not let anything deprive you of this sweet definition of Christ, which brings joy even to the angels in heaven (LW 26:38)

Opening Prayer

L: Jesus Christ is the propitiation for our sins,

P: And not for ours only but also for the sins of the whole world. (1 John 2:2)

L: This is good, and it is pleasing in the sight of God our Savior,

P: Who desires all people to be saved and to come to the knowledge of the truth. (1 Timothy 2:3–4)

L: Open our eyes, O Lord, that we may behold wondrous things out of Your Word.

P: Amen!

Sovereign God

Have participants work in pairs to complete this section, then review with the whole group. The most basic theological idea in Calvinism is that God is sovereign. In fact, God's sovereignty is regarded as His chief attribute—His chief characteristic—out of which flow all His actions toward His creation.

Compare the Bible verses below. What differences can you see between them?

The first group of verses emphasizes God's sovereignty, lordship, and almighty power.

Exodus 20:1–6—God has the power both to command obedience and to punish those who refuse to obey. God will not share His sovereignty and power with anyone or anything.

2 Chronicles 20:6—God reigns supreme over "all the kingdoms of the nations." He has all power and might, against which no one can stand.

Psalm 103:19—God's kingdom rules over all things.

1 Timothy 6:15–16—God "is the blessed and only Sovereign, the King of kings and Lord of lords, who alone has immortality, [and] dwells in unapproachable light." The second group of verses emphasizes God's mercy, forbearance, and forgiving love.

Psalm 103:8—God is "merciful and gracious, slow to anger and abounding in steadfast love."

Joel 2:12–13—The Lord loves to show compassion and mercy to those who repent of their sins. (This text quotes Psalm 103.)

Ephesians 2:4–5—God is "rich in mercy" and full of "great love" that acts on our behalf even when we are dead in trespasses and sins.

1 John 4:16—"God is love."

According to the following verses, which of God's attributes seems to be His dominant attribute—His sovereignty or His mercy? Stated another way, what is God's favorite way of acting toward His creation?

Ezekiel 18:23—God does not desire the death of the sinner. Rather, God desires, more than anything else, to show mercy.

Hosea 6:1–3—God's sovereignty, shown by His tearing and striking, is really only the servant of His mercy: "He has torn us, that He may heal us; He has struck us down, and He will bind us up."

Jonah 3:10—God turned back from destroying Nineveh.

Discuss: *What difference does it make whether God acts primarily according to His sovereignty or primarily according to His mercy? Which of His attributes would you like Him to follow when He is dealing with you?* (By way of analogy, you could raise the issue of parents. Would you like to have parents who act arbitrarily toward you, so that you never know whether they are going to treat you kindly or harshly, or would you rather have the certainty that their fundamental attitude toward you is one of compassion and love?)

Discuss: *Which of God's attributes—His sovereignty or His mercy—gives you the most certainty of your forgiveness of sins and salvation?* (If sovereignty is God's chief attribute, then He is free to act in any way He wishes. In fact, He could act in a totally arbitrary way and be justified in doing so. In that case, however, how could you ever be certain of His promises of forgiveness and salvation? However, when mercy is regarded as God's chief attribute, you can be certain of your salvation, never doubting that all your sins are fully forgiven. It is part of God's nature to forgive and to show mercy, and God really does not want to act against His own nature!)

No Limits

Complete this section with the whole group. Calvinism's concept of limited atonement (that Christ died only for some people, not for all people of all time) rises out of the emphasis on the sovereignty of God. Essentially, the logic (faulty as it is) goes like this: because God is sovereign and has complete control over everything, it is not possible to act outside of His will. If someone should reject God's grace in Christ and be damned, it must be because God willed for this person—and predestined this person—to be damned.

In what way do these Bible verses speak against Calvinism's idea that Christ died only for some, but not for all people of all time?

John 3:16–17—God so loved the world that He gave His only Son.

John 6:51—Jesus' body, crucified on the cross, is for the life of the world.

1 Timothy 2:4—God desires all people to be saved.

1 John 2:2—Christ is the propitiation (that is, the atoning sacrifice) for the sins of the whole world.

Discuss: *Because Christ died for all people of all time, does that mean that all people of all time will go to heaven? Use Romans 3:21–26 and Ephesians 2:8–9 to guide your discussion.* (Christ died for all people, and in Him, all sins are totally and completely forgiven. However, not all people will receive the benefits of Christ's forgiveness, because some refuse to believe. An analogy would be the prisoner to whom the jailer says, "Go, you have been set free." That prisoner is totally free, even though he or she might foolishly say, "I don't want that freedom. I am staying right here in my cell." In the same way, Christ's blood is for the forgiveness of all sins of all people for all time. However, there are many people, like the foolish prisoner, who say, "I don't need Your forgiveness, Jesus.")

What do the following Bible verses say about predestination?

Romans 8:29–30—God foreknew and predestined you for salvation, having called you and justified you by the power of Christ's death and resurrection.

Ephesians 1:5, 11—God predestined us when He adopted us in Baptism. That is to say, because we are baptized, we are certainly and without doubt His children and heirs of eternal life.

Note: The term *predestined* is a name that applies only to Christians. The name does not apply to unbelievers, as Calvinism claims. For an excellent treatment of predestination, read the Epitome of the Formula of Concord, Article XI, "God's Eternal Foreknowledge and Election."

Discuss: *How do you personally know you are predestined? Stated another way, to what can you look for certainty and assurance of your predestination for heaven?* (Because Christ died for all people, and because Christ's death and resurrection are delivered to you through preaching, Baptism, Absolution, and the Lord's Supper, these gifts provide you with ongoing assurances that you shall not fail to be with Jesus with you leave this life.)

Closing Prayer

Almighty, everlasting God, Your Son has assured forgiveness of sins and deliverance from eternal death. Strengthen us by Your Holy Spirit that our faith in Christ may increase daily and that we may hold fast to the hope that on the Last Day we shall be raised in glory to eternal life; through Jesus Christ, our Lord. Amen. (*LSB*, p. 313)

4 Presbyterians

A Message from Martin Luther

Especially practice this pronoun "our" in such a way that this syllable, once believed, may swallow up and absorb all your sins, that is, that you may be certain that Christ has taken away not only the sins of some men but your sins and those of the whole world. . . . That is, believe that Christ was given not only for the sins of others but also for yours. Hold to this firmly, and do not let anything deprive you of this sweet definition of Christ, which brings joy even to the angels in heaven. (LW 26:38)

Opening Prayer

L: Jesus Christ is the propitiation for our sins,

P: And not for ours only but also for the sins of the whole world. (1 John 2:2)

L: This is good, and it is pleasing in the sight of God our Savior,

P: Who desires all people to be saved and to come to the knowledge of the truth.
(1 Timothy 2:3–4)

L: Open our eyes, O Lord, that we may behold wondrous things out of Your Word.

P: Amen!

Sovereign God

Compare the Bible verses in the left colum with those in the right column. What differences can you see between them?

Exodus 20:1–6	Psalm 103:8
2 Chronicles 20:6	Joel 2:12–13
Psalm 103:19	Ephesians 2:4–5
1 Timothy 6:15–16	1 John 4:16

According to the following verses, which of God's attributes seems to be His dominant attribute—His sovereignty or His mercy? Stated another way, what is God's favorite way of acting toward His creation?

Ezekiel 18:23

Hosea 6:1–3

Jonah 3:10

What difference does it make whether God acts primarily according to His sovereignty or primarily according to His mercy? Which of His attributes would you like Him to follow when He is dealing with you?

Which of God's attributes—His sovereignty or His mercy—gives you the most certainty of your forgiveness of sins and salvation?

No Limits

In what way do these Bible verses speak against Calvinism's idea that Christ died only for some, but not for all people of all time?

John 3:16–17

John 6:51

1 Timothy 2:4

1 John 2:2

Because Christ died for all people of all time, does that mean that all people of all time will go to heaven? Use **Romans 3:21–26** and **Ephesians 2:8–9** to guide your discussion.

What do the following Bible verses say about predestination?

Romans 8:29–30

Ephesians 1:5, 11

How do you personally know you are predestined? Stated another way, to what can you look for certainty and assurance of your predestination for heaven?

 One Christ, Many Creeds copyright © 2008 Concordia Publishing House. Scripture: ESV* Luther's Works, American Edition: vol. 26 copyright © 1963 Concordia Publishing House. All rights reserved. Reproduced by permission.

5

Christian Reformed

© iStockphoto/Justin McD

Lesson Focus

In Christ, we have a sure salvation; eternal life with Him is certain. In this session, we focus primarily on the perseverance of the saints, an element of John Calvin's theology that creates not merely uncertainty, but false hope.

Historical Context

The name *Reformed* is an umbrella term for those church bodies that separated from Roman Catholicism during the Reformation in the sixteenth century but were not Lutheran. John Calvin's theology provided the cornerstone of historic Reformed teachings, but other theological influences included Ulrich Zwingli and Martin Luther's close friend and colleague, Philip Melanchthon. Major historical writings that describe the teachings of the Reformed church bodies are the Belgic Confession (1561), the Heidelberg Catechism (1562), and the Canons of Dort (adopted at a synod meeting in Holland from 1618–19). The Canons of Dort are particularly important for this group's rejection of the teachings of Jacobus Arminius and its confirmation of the principles of Calvinism.

Reformed church bodies came to America primarily through Dutch and German immigration. While there are various Reformed groups in the United States today, the sample group studied here is the Christian Reformed, a group formed by Dutch immigrants in 1857 that was originally named the True Holland Reformed Church. Separated by great distance from its parent church body in Holland, this group took issue with the Dutch Reformed Church over several matters of doctrine and discipline. Despite these differences, however, the Christian Reformed Church today remains primarily a Calvinist church body.

Distribute copies of Participant Page 5. Have participants read through the quote from the Confessions and continue with the responsive prayer. You may also choose to distribute copies of the Quick Comparison Chart for this lesson at this time.

A Message from the Lutheran Confessions

Many "hear the word, receive it with joy. But these have no root; they believe for a while, and in time of testing fall away" (Luke 8:13). The reason is not that God was unwilling to grant grace for perseverance to those in whom He "began a good work," for that is contrary to St. Paul (Philippians 1:6). The reason is that they willfully turn away again from the holy commandment, grieve and embitter the Holy Spirit, involve themselves again in the world's filth, and redecorate their hearts as homes for the devil. For them their last situation is worse than the first. (SD XI 42)

Opening Prayer

L: For if, after they have escaped the defilements of the world through the knowledge of our Lord and Savior Jesus Christ, they are again entangled in them and overcome,

P: **The last state has become worse for them than the first.** (2 Peter 2:20)

L: The God of all grace, who has called you to His eternal glory in Christ, will Himself restore, confirm, strengthen, and establish you.

P: **To Him be the dominion forever and ever.** (1 Peter 5:10–11)

L: Open our eyes, O Lord, that we may behold wondrous things out of Your Word.

P: **Amen!**

Persevere

Read the suggested Scriptures and complete this section together. Just as Calvinism's limited atonement flows from its emphasis on the sovereignty of God (see session 4), so also does the idea of the perseverance of the saints flow from the concept of limited atonement. If God planned from eternity that you will be saved (that is, He planned from eternity to make you one of the lucky ones for whom Christ died), then you are going to be saved no matter what. Stated another way, once you are saved, you are always saved—God's sovereignty cannot be violated!

In what way do the following Bible verses cast a question on the Calvinist teaching of the perseverance of the saints?

Luke 8:13—"They believe for a while, and in time of testing fall away."

1 Timothy 4:1–2—"Some will depart from the faith."

2 Peter 2:20–21—"After knowing it [they] turn back from the holy commandment delivered to them."

Discuss: *What dangerous temptations can be created by the Calvinist teaching of the perseverance of the saints?* (The Calvinist doctrine of the perseverance of the saints teaches you to live in false security. If you are "once saved, always saved," there remains no need for hearing the Word, receiving the Lord's Supper, or even repenting of sins!)

Discuss: *In what way might the Calvinist teaching of the perseverance of the saints make the Sixth Petition of the Lord's Prayer (Matthew 6:13) into a useless prayer?* (According to the Small Catechism's explanation of the Sixth Petition, we pray "that God would guard us and keep us so that the devil, the world, and our sinful nature may not deceive us or mislead us into false belief, despair, and other great shame and vice" [p. 195]. But these temptations really are not a serious threat to our salvation and eternal life if the Calvinist teaching of the perseverance of the saints is true.)

Discuss: *In what way might the Calvinist teaching of the perseverance of the saints tempt you to take your faith's focus off Jesus' death and resurrection for your forgiveness and eternal life? Stated another way, in what way does the perseverance of the saints tempt you to stop trusting in God day by day?* (The perseverance of the saints tempts you to live any way you want to live, rather than by repentance and trust in Jesus. The Calvinist doctrines of the perseverance of the saints and the limited atonement teach that nothing really matters in your life; you were predestined from eternity, and it is impossible to fall away.)

Safety

Have participants complete this section on their own. If we reject the Calvinist teaching of the perseverance of the saints, it does not mean that God's people have no protection or safety! Rather, God promises great protection for His people.

In what way do the following Bible verses assure you of God's continued care and protection for all eternity?

Galatians 3:27—In Baptism, you have been clothed with Christ, who has now become your strong defense and armor against those things that would seek to pull you away from the faith.

Romans 8:31–39—"If God is for us, who can be against us?" Not even the strongest powers of death and hell can overcome those whose faith is in Christ alone.

1 Peter 1:3–5—You are "by God's power being guarded through faith."

Discuss: *If certainty of forgiveness and salvation cannot be found in the Calvinist teaching of the perseverance of the saints, where shall we look to find it?* (Certainty and assurance are not found in a concept, such as the perseverance of the saints, which takes your eyes off Christ, but in Christ alone.)

Closing Prayer

O holy and most merciful God, You have taught us the way of Your commandments. We implore You to pour out Your grace into our hearts. Cause it to bear fruit in us that, being ever mindful of Your mercies and Your laws, we may always be directed to Your will and daily increase in love toward You and one another. Enable us to resist all evil and to live a godly life. Help us to follow the example of our Lord and Savior, Jesus Christ, and to walk in His steps until we shall possess the kingdom that has been prepared for us in heaven; through Jesus Christ, our Lord. (*LSB*, p. 308)

5 Christian Reformed

A Message from the Lutheran Confessions

Many "hear the word, receive it with joy. But these have no root; they believe for a while, and in time of testing fall away" (Luke 8:13). The reason is not that God was unwilling to grant grace for perseverance to those in whom He "began a good work," for that is contrary to St. Paul (Philippians 1:6). The reason is that they willfully turn away again from the holy commandment, grieve and embitter the Holy Spirit, involve themselves again in the world's filth, and redecorate their hearts as homes for the devil. For them their last situation is worse than the first. (SD XI 42)

Opening Prayer

L: For if, after they have escaped the defilements of the world through the knowledge of our Lord and Savior Jesus Christ, they are again entangled in them and overcome,

P: **The last state has become worse for them than the first.** (2 Peter 2:20)

L: The God of all grace, who has called you to His eternal glory in Christ, will Himself restore, confirm, strengthen, and establish you.

P: **To Him be the dominion forever and ever.** (1 Peter 5:10–11)

L: Open our eyes, O Lord, that we may behold wondrous things out of Your Word.

P: **Amen!**

Persevere

In what way do the following Bible verses cast a question on the Calvinist teaching of the perseverance of the saints?

Luke 8:13
_____

1 Timothy 4:1–2
_____

2 Peter 2:20–21
_____

What dangerous temptations can be created by the Calvinist teaching of the perseverance of the saints?

_____

In what way might the Calvinist teaching of the perseverance of the saints make the Sixth Petition of the Lord's Prayer (**Matthew 6:13**) into a useless prayer?

_____

In what way might the Calvinist teaching of the perseverance of the saints tempt you to take your faith's focus off Jesus' death and resurrection for your forgiveness and eternal life? Stated another way, in what way does the perseverance of the saints tempt you to stop trusting in God day by day?

_____

_____

_____

Safety

In what way do the following Bible verses assure you of God's continued care and protection for all eternity?

Galatians 3:27
_____

Romans 8:31–39
_____

1 Peter 1:3–5
_____

If certainty of forgiveness and salvation cannot be found in the Calvinist teaching of the perseverance of the saints, where shall we look to find it?

_____

_____

Participant Page 5 *One Christ, Many Creeds* copyright © 2008 Concordia Publishing House. Scripture: ESV® *Concordia: The Lutheran Confessions,* second edition, copyright © 2006 Concordia Publishing House. All rights reserved. Reproduced by permission.

6

Anglicans/ Episcopalians

Lesson Focus

In Christ, we have a sure salvation; eternal life with Him is certain. In this session, we focus primarily on the Anglican/Episcopalian accent on form over theology.

Historical Context

It may seem odd to place the Anglicans/ Episcopalians in the category of Calvinist church bodies. The Anglican/Episcopalian churches share liturgical roots with the other ancient churches. They also have retained a sacramental system very similar to that of Rome. However, Anglican/Puritan settlers who came to the New World were greatly influenced by the work of Calvin. Thus the Anglican/Episcopal churches gave rise to the Calvinist churches in North America.

The Protestant Episcopal Church in the U.S.A. is part of a larger community called the Anglican Communion, which recognizes the leadership of the Archbishop of Canterbury, England. (There are other Anglican and Episcopal churches in countries formerly part of the British Empire.) The Anglican Communion traces its history to the sixteenth century, when King Henry VIII of England clashed with Pope Clement VII over the matter of Henry's divorce. This clash ultimately led to the establishment the Church of England, distinct from the Roman Catholic Church.

The Church of England came to the United States by means of immigration, the first congregation being founded in Jamestown in 1607. After the War of Independence, the Episcopal Church became established in the United States as its own organization. Both Anglicans and Episcopalians use the Book of Common Prayer in a manner similar to the way Lutherans use the Small Catechism and the Book of Concord.

Various theologians have influenced the Anglicans and Episcopalians, including Martin Luther, John Calvin, and the Swiss reformer Ulrich Zwingli. Roman Catholic roots remain evident. This gathering of various teachings has led to a situation in which the outward form of worship provides greater unity than specific doctrinal teachings. Wide variations in teaching are tolerated, so long as a general unity in worship is maintained in one of two general categories: a "high liturgy," in which worship is elaborate and ornate (reflecting ancient roots), or a "low liturgy" of a simpler, plainer style (reflecting the influence of John Calvin).

Hand out copies of Participant Page 6 along with the Quick Comparison Chart, and work through the lesson together.

© Shutterstock/Patrick Tolley

A Message from Martin Luther

Without the Holy Spirit and without grace man can do nothing but sin and so goes on endlessly from sin to sin. But when there is also this added element that he does not uphold sound doctrine, rejects the Word of salvation, and resists the Holy Spirit, then, with the support of his free will, he also becomes an enemy of God, blasphemes the Holy Spirit, and completely follows the evil desires of his heart. (LW 2:40)

Opening Prayer

L: Exhort one another every day, as long as it is called "today,"

P: **That none of you may be hardened by the deceitfulness of sin.**

L: For we share in Christ, if indeed we hold our original confidence firm to the end.

P: **As it is said, "Today, if you hear His voice, do not harden your hearts as in the rebellion."** (Hebrews 3:13–15)

L: Open our eyes, O Lord, that we may behold wondrous things out of Your Word.

P: **Amen!**

One in Worship

One of the main features of Anglican/Episcopalian church bodies is their focus on a common form of worship, even at the expense of common teachings or beliefs.

What do the following Bible verses have to say about concerning oneself with a common form of worship, but not concerning oneself with the content of teaching or belief?

Isaiah 29:13—Through Isaiah, God lamented that His people "draw near with their mouth and honor Me with their lips, while their hearts are far from Me." With these words, God warns that true worship is not merely a matter of maintaining outward ceremonies and observances.

Mark 7:1–8—Citing the previous passage from Isaiah, Jesus condemns the Pharisees and scribes for concerning themselves more with the form and performance of their ceremonies than with keeping "the commandment of God."

2 Timothy 3:1–5—Paul warns Timothy against those who wish to maintain an "appearance of godliness, but denying its power."

Discuss: *What false sense of assurance or certainty can you fall into if the main emphasis is on outward form rather than the content of your faith?* (Emphasis on the outward form or performance of your faith at the expense of holding fast in your heart to what you believe will create the impression that you are saved by what you do, rather than by what you believe. When the outward form of worship is the main emphasis, you can feel tempted to believe whatever you want to believe, so long as you perform the prescribed acts of worship correctly.)

Discuss: *What can we say about the form of worship? Does form matter at all, or is anything permissible so long as we believe the Christian faith rightly? Compare Mark 2:27–28 and 2 Timothy 4:3 for guidance in your discussion.* (Some people might think that since worship forms are not spelled out and required by the teachings of the Bible, any form of worship will be fine. After all, "The Sabbath was made for man, not man for the Sabbath" [Mark 2:27]. While these words are very true, it does not follow from them that any and every form of worship is equally beneficial or worthy of use. Worship forms will want to consistently reflect the deepest levels of faith and faithfulness to the Word. Worship forms will not want to run after the whims of the surrounding culture, because "the time is coming when people will not endure sound teaching, but having itching ears they will accumulate for themselves teachers to suit their own passions" [2 Timothy 4:3]. Some of these passions—or emotions—might prove to be counterproductive to proclaiming and hearing the life-giving Word of God.

The Lutheran Confessions strike this balance in this way:

We believe, teach, and confess that the community of God . . . has the power to change such worship ceremonies in a way that may be most useful and edifying to the community of God. Nevertheless, all frivolity and offense should be avoided in this matter. [FC Ep X 4–5])

One in Faith

The emphasis on common worship forms at the expense of common belief has led the Anglican/Episcopalian church bodies into many teachings and practices that may be rejected by more conservative denominations. These teachings and practices include both the acceptance of the practice of homosexuality and of women's ordination. This means that the Anglican/Episcopalian church bodies have sacrificed the teachings of God's Word for the sake of maintaining an outward unity based on form.

In what way does Matthew 23:27–28 speak a strong warning and condemnation to every Christian? (Jesus warns against a Christianity that concerns itself only with its outward show, yet is dead inside because of a refusal to listen and believe God's Word, the Bible. Daily surrounded and tempted by the devil, the world, and our own sinful [self-centered] nature, Christians are continually tempted to pick and choose their favorite parts of God's Word while rejecting other parts as unacceptable. When we give in and fall prey to such temptations, says Jesus, we join those of old who "murdered the prophets" [v. 31] because they did not like the messages the prophets proclaimed.)

Discuss: *When a church body becomes tolerant and accepting of the teachings and practices of the world rather than of the Bible, what impact does this have on the people in the pews? Does this mean that everyone who attends such a church is therefore an unbeliever?* (Faith comes through hearing the Word of God [Romans 10:17]. When the Word of God is not proclaimed, how can the people believe? Yet, even in a church body where "anything goes," if God's Bible is still read in their midst, then God powerfully and miraculously creates believers, often in spite of what the church body as a whole believes.)

Discuss: *What things would you be willing to give up, and what things would you insist on keeping, in order to maintain the unity of your church body? What things should be considered nonnegotiable?* (In the end, every sacrifice that could possibly be required of us would be worth making, so long as we do not give up the clear teachings of God's Word, the Bible. The Christian faith as it is taught in the Scriptures and the Lutheran Confessions should be regarded as nonnegotiable because God's Word brings eternal life. Without God's Word, there is only darkness and death.)

Closing Prayer

Almighty and most gracious God and Father, we implore you to turn the hearts of all who have forsaken the faith once delivered to Your Church, especially those who have wandered from it or are in doubt through the corruption of Your truth. Mercifully visit and restore them that in gladness of heart they may take pleasure in Your Word and be made wise to salvation through faith in Your Son, Jesus Christ, our Lord. Amen. (*LSB*, p. 306)

6 Anglicans/Episcopalians

A Message from Martin Luther

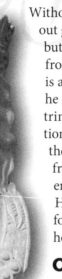

Without the Holy Spirit and without grace man can do nothing but sin and so goes on endlessly from sin to sin. But when there is also this added element that he does not uphold sound doctrine, rejects the Word of salvation, and resists the Holy Spirit, then, with the support of his free will, he also becomes an enemy of God, blasphemes the Holy Spirit, and completely follows the evil desires of his heart. (LW 2:40)

Opening Prayer

L: Exhort one another every day, as long as it is called "today,"

P: That none of you may be hardened by the deceitfulness of sin.

L: For we share in Christ, if indeed we hold our original confidence firm to the end.

P: As it is said, "Today, if you hear His voice, do not harden your hearts as in the rebellion." (Hebrews 3:13–15)

L: Open our eyes, O Lord, that we may behold wondrous things out of Your Word.

P: Amen!

One in Worship

What do the following Bible verses have to say about concerning oneself with a common form of worship, but not concerning oneself with the content of teaching or belief?

Isaiah 29:13

Mark 7:1–8

2 Timothy 3:1–5

What false sense of assurance or certainty can you fall into if the main emphasis is on outward form rather than the content of your faith?

What can we say about the form of worship? Does form matter at all, or is anything permissible so long as we believe the Christian faith rightly? Compare **Mark 2:27–28** and **2 Timothy 4:3** for guidance in your discussion.

One in Faith

In what way does **Matthew 23:27–28** speak a strong warning and condemnation to every Christian?

When a church body becomes tolerant and accepting of the teachings and practices of the world rather than of the Bible, what impact does this have on the people in the pews? Does this mean that everyone who attends such a church is therefore an unbeliever?

What things would you be willing to give up, and what things would you insist on keeping, in order to maintain the unity of your church body? What things should be considered non-negotiable?

Participant Page 6 *One Christ, Many Creeds* copyright © 2008 Concordia Publishing House. Scripture: ESV® Luther's Works, American Edition: vol. 2 copyright © 1960 Concordia Publishing House. All rights reserved. Reproduced by permission.

Unit III
Arminian Church Bodies

Methodists
Salvation Army
Church of the Nazarene

General Introduction

A native of Holland, Jacobus Arminius (1560–1609) studied theology in Calvinist Geneva. However, after Arminius returned home to Holland in 1587, his study of St. Paul's Epistle to the Romans led him to doubt whether Calvin's teaching on predestination was correct. (Calvin taught double predestination, which means that God predestined some people for salvation and others for damnation.) This doubt about one of Calvin's teachings soon grew into opposition to most of Calvin's theology.

Arminian teachings were formally set forth in a document called the Remonstrance of 1610, written one year after Arminius had died. This document, which gives an answer to many points in Calvin's theology, was not warmly accepted in Holland, the home of those Calvinists called the Dutch Reformed. The Dutch Reformed Church condemned Arminianism at the Synod of Dort (1618–1619).

Arminianism opposed all five chief points of John Calvin's theology, as shown below.

Where Calvin taught . . .	Arminianism taught . . .
Total depravity of man	Man is *not* totally depraved, but has a free will.
Unconditional election	Election is God's response to your personal decision to follow Him.
Limited atonement	Christ died potentially for everyone, so long as you decide to accept Him.
Irresistible grace	Grace is completely resistible and is based on personal choice.
Perseverance of the saints	You can walk away from salvation any time you like.

The three major Arminian church bodies included in this unit do not date to the days of Jacobus Arminius. In the 1700s, more than a hundred years after Arminius died, the early Methodists discovered in Arminianism an answer to their dissatisfaction with Calvinism in England. The Salvation Army and The Church of the Nazarene subsequently grew out of Methodism.

7

Methodists

Lesson Focus

In Christ, we have a sure salvation; eternal life with Him is certain. In this session we focus primarily on the Arminian teaching of free will, which teaches you to trust in yourself to some degree rather than trusting exclusively in your Lord Jesus Christ's death and resurrection for you.

Historical Context

Methodism traces its history to the leadership and teachings of John Wesley (1703–1791) and his brother Charles (1707–1788), who were born and raised in the Church of England (Anglican). John Wesley experienced a strange warming of his heart on May 24, 1738, when he listened to a public reading of Martin Luther's *Preface to Romans*. Later calling this experience a conversion that had been caused by the Holy Spirit, John Wesley and his brother fostered a movement that emphasized a warmer, more heartfelt religion than he had learned from the strict liturgical worship forms of the Church of England.

The emphasis on heartfelt religion led to the development of a church body that today continues to focus more on human care and neighborly compassion than on faithfulness to a particular set of theological teachings. Because free will remains a major theological emphasis in Methodism, a wide variety of theological opinions and practices can be found coexisting in the United Methodist Church of today. Stated another way, the specific teachings of the Christian faith are not nearly as important to Methodism as is the practice of love in actions toward one's neighbor. The best Christian life is lived according to a certain method (hence the name *Methodism*) by which the Christian focuses on moral self-improvement and eventual perfection through service to others.

Distribute copies of Participant Page 7 and work through the lesson together with the whole group. You may also want to distribute copies of the Quick Comparison Chart at this time.

A Message from Martin Luther

In worldly and outward affairs, which apply to the livelihood and maintenance of the body, a person is cunning, intelligent, and quite active. But in spiritual and divine things, which apply to the salvation of the soul, a person is like a pillar of salt, like Lot's wife [Genesis 19:26], indeed, like a log and stone. He is like a lifeless statue, which uses neither eyes nor mouth, neither sense nor heart. (SD II 20)

Opening Prayer

L: I do not understand my own actions. For I do not do what I want, but I do the very thing I hate. (Romans 7:15)

P: **I know that nothing good dwells in me, that is, in my flesh.** (Romans 7:18)

L: Who will deliver me from this body of death?

P: **Thanks be to God through Jesus Christ our Lord!** (Romans 7:24–25)

L: Open our eyes, O Lord, that we may behold wondrous things out of Your Word.

P: **Amen!**

© Shutterstock/Brasiliao-media

Free Will

Why are some people saved and others not? Calvinism's limited atonement attempts to give an answer based on the idea of God's sovereignty. Arminianism answers in the opposite way, pointing to the idea of the freedom of the human will. According to Arminian teaching, you personally choose whether or not you wish to be saved.

Discuss: *In what areas of life do people have the free exercise of their will? Are there any areas in life in which free will is limited or restricted in some way?* (Free will is exercised in what might be called the physical aspects of life. People exercise free will when deciding what to eat, what to wear, where to live, and so on. But even in physical matters, the human will is not entirely free. For example, a child's free will is limited by his or her parent's rules, and a citizen's free will is limited by the government's laws. Free will is also limited by many different circumstances such as the economy [you cannot go to work if there are no jobs available], the weather [it is hard to sunbathe in a blizzard], and the limitations of the physical body [a person who is allergic to bee stings might not want to be a beekeeper].

The point of the discussion is that even in everyday matters, the freedom of the will is more of an ideal than a practical reality. If the human will faces so many limitations in physical things, how much more is this the case in spiritual things?)

What do the following Bible verses have to say about the freedom of the will when it comes to spiritual matters?

Romans 8:7—The sinful mind is "hostile to God." In its enmity and hatred toward God, the sinful mind cannot choose to be God's friend.

Galatians 5:17—"The desires of the flesh are against the Spirit." Stated another way, the sinful flesh is not free to choose its desires. The flesh only desires the opposite of what the Spirit desires.

Ephesians 2:1—Far from having a free will, our will in spiritual matters is "dead in the trespasses and sins."

The preceding verses make it clear that the human will is bound and cannot act freely in spiritual matters. Since this is so, how is it possible even to believe in God, according to the following verses?

Romans 10:17—When we believe in Jesus for salvation, it is not because we have exercised our free will in choosing Him, but because God has planted His miraculous gift of faith within us through the hearing of the Word.

2 Corinthians 4:6—Where the heart is only darkness and evil (compare Matthew 15:19–20), God has caused His light to shine in the darkness through the hearing of His Word.

Ephesians 2:8–9—We are not saved by our choice, but by faith, which is "the gift of God."

John 11:38–44—This section of Scripture serves as an analogy. Lazarus did not exercise his free will in listening to Jesus' call and command. The powerful Word of God raised Lazarus up from the dead, so that he was able to respond to Jesus' voice. In the same way, we do not follow Jesus as an exercise of our free will, but we follow Him as a result of the miraculous work of His Word, which raises us up from the death of our sins.

What do the following verses say about those to whom God has given His miraculous gift of faith?

Psalm 51:10—God miraculously creates "a clean heart" and "a right spirit" when He gives the gift of faith.

Romans 7:15–19—The new heart and will go to war against the old, dead, stubborn heart and will. Christians still do not have free exercise of their will in spiritual matters, as shown by Paul's example.

Discuss: *The Bible makes it clear that salvation is entirely God's work, to which no human being adds anything, "so that no one may boast" (Ephesians 2:9). The Bible also teaches that when a person goes to hell, it is that person's own hardness of heart and unbelief that caused it. In what way do these two teachings from the Bible seem contradictory and illogical? Can you* think of any other teachings from the Bible that also seem contradictory and illogical? (Answers may vary. Logically speaking, if a person is to be blamed for his or her own condemnation, he or she ought to be credited with his or her own salvation. But the Bible teaches that only God gets the credit for salvation, working though Christ. This illogical teaching is not the only mystery of the faith. Equally illogical are the teachings of the Trinity, the two natures of Christ, the presence of Christ in Holy Communion, and so on. The point of the discussion is that human logic does not determine the faith, but the Bible does.)

Discuss: *In what way can an emphasis on the freedom of the human will, which is contrary to the teachings of the Bible, cause you to doubt your forgiveness and salvation?* (Can you ever be sure you have exerted yourself enough to qualify for eternal life? Can you be certain that your decision or your personal commitment was sufficiently sincere and heartfelt to ensure your salvation?)

Heartfelt

Have participants work in pairs for this section. Review as one large group. The focus on heartfelt religion promoted by the Wesleys led Methodism to emphasize Christian love as being more important than Christian truth. Stated another way, Methodism emphasizes the importance of helping the neighbor in need more than it does specific points of teaching.

According to the following Bible verses, what is the relationship between truth and love?

Zechariah 8:19—God calls upon His people to love His truth.

Ephesians 4:15; John 17:17—God's Word is truth, the truth that love prompts us to speak.

1 Peter 1:22—Obedience to the truth and love for neighbor are not separated, but are set together in harmony.

Discuss: *What might be some of the dangers of creating too much separation between truth and love? Where might an emphasis on truth at the expense of love lead you? Where might an emphasis on love at the expense of truth lead you?* (Focusing on the truth without love and

forbearance can lead to legalistic demands. Focusing on love at the expense of the truth is really no love at all. It is just a warm, fuzzy feeling that is powerless.)

What does Matthew 13:23 say about the source of our works of love toward our neighbor? (The one and only source of love for our neighbor is the seed of God's Word, which is sown in us and produces a rich harvest within us.)

According to the following Bible passages, is it right for Christians to attend themselves only to God's Word and to ignore their neighbor's needs?

James 2:14–17—Faith without works is dead.

1 John 3:18—Love for neighbor is tied both to serving the neighbor's need and to God's Word of truth.

Discuss: *If your circumstances forced you into the difficult position of needing to choose between giving your neighbor consolation from God's Word or helping in his or her physical need, which would you choose? Why? Use Acts 3:1–6 to help guide your discussion.* (The apostles had no money, but they had something greater: God's Word. Caring for our neighbor's physical need is good, but it only serves the neighbor for this life. Speaking God's Word to the neighbor serves him or her both in this life and in the life to come.)

Closing Prayer

Almighty God, You have called Your Church to witness that in Christ You have reconciled us to Yourself. Grant that by Your Holy Spirit we may proclaim the good news of Your salvation so that all who hear it may receive the gift of salvation; through Jesus Christ, our Lord. Amen. (*LSB*, p. 305)

7 Methodists

A Message from Martin Luther

In worldly and outward affairs, which apply to the livelihood and maintenance of the body, a person is cunning, intelligent, and quite active. But in spiritual and divine things, which apply to the salvation of the soul, a person is like a pillar of salt, like Lot's wife [Genesis 19:26], indeed, like a log and stone. He is like a lifeless statue, which uses neither eyes nor mouth, neither sense nor heart. (SD II 20)

Opening Prayer

L: I do not understand my own actions. For I do not do what I want, but I do the very thing I hate. (Romans 7:15)

P: **I know that nothing good dwells in me, that is, in my flesh.** (Romans 7:18)

L: Who will deliver me from this body of death?

P: **Thanks be to God through Jesus Christ our Lord!** (Romans 7:24–25)

L: Open our eyes, O Lord, that we may behold wondrous things out of Your Word.

P: **Amen!**

Free Will

In what areas of life do people have the free exercise of their will? Are there any areas in life in which free will is limited or restricted in some way?

What do the following Bible verses have to say about the freedom of the will when it comes to spiritual matters?

Romans 8:7

Galatians 5:17

Ephesians 2:1

The preceding verses make it clear that the human will is bound and cannot act freely in spiritual matters. Since this is so, how is it possible even to believe in God, according to the following verses?

Romans 10:17

2 Corinthians 4:6

Ephesians 2:8–9

John 11:38–44

What do the following verses say about those to whom God has given His miraculous gift of faith?

Psalm 51:10

Romans 7:15–19

Heartfelt

According to the following Bible verses, what is the relationship between truth and love?

Zechariah 8:19

Ephesians 4:15; John 17:17

1 Peter 1:22

What might be some of the dangers of creating too much separation between truth and love? Where might an emphasis on truth at the expense of love lead you? Where might an emphasis on love at the expense of truth lead you?

What does **Matthew 13:23** say about the source of our works of love toward our neighbor?

According to the following Bible passages, is it right for Christians to attend themselves only to God's Word and to ignore their neighbor's needs?

James 2:14–17

1 John 3:18

If your circumstances forced you into the difficult position of needing to choose between giving your neighbor consolation from God's Word or helping in his or her physical need, which would you choose? Why?

Use **Acts 3:1–6** to help guide your discussion.

© 2008 Concordia Publishing House. Scripture: ESV* *Concordia: The Lutheran Confessions*, second edition, copyright © 2006 Concordia Publishing House. All rights reserved. Reproduced by permission.

8
Salvation Army

Lesson Focus

In Christ, we have a sure salvation; eternal life with Him is certain. In this session, we focus primarily on the Arminian teaching of election as God's response to your personal decision. This teaching, like the Arminian teaching of free will, likewise teaches you to trust in yourself to some degree rather than trusting exclusively in your Lord Jesus Christ's death and resurrection for you.

Historical Context

The Salvation Army is a daughter of Methodism, founded by a Methodist preacher named William Booth (1829–1912). Booth exemplified the Methodist tendency to focus on the human care of the most impoverished and neglected people. He developed many new methods for reaching out to the poor in inner-city London, including street preaching and Christian marching bands. Many of the poorest people in London found food, shelter, and compassion in the Christian missions that had been established by Booth and his wife. When many enthusiastic followers began to join Booth's labors, they were named the Salvation Army, which ranked and grouped workers in a structure patterned after the British military.

The basic teachings of the Salvation Army were formulated in its Foundation Deed (1878). As an Arminian church body, it emphasizes the role of personal decision making in the Christian life. Sanctification is not so much what Christ has done for you, but what you personally choose to do for Christ, whom you serve by serving your neighbor. Stated another way, the Salvation Army holds (along with the Methodists and all other Arminian bodies) that sanctification is something you see happening in your life as a result of your own personal efforts, rather than something that you believe by faith.

Many people today associate the Salvation Army with the bell ringers who stand outside stores during the Christmas season. The funds collected from this effort are used almost exclusively for the poor.

Distribute copies of Participant Page 8 along with the Quick Comparison Chart, and complete the opening activities.

A Message from Martin Luther

Christ Himself explains how He wants the words "No longer do I call you servants, but I call you My friends" to be understood. He says: "This friendship—the fact that I call you My friends—you do not have from yourselves; you have it because I chose you as friends through My suffering and death. . . ." This blasts and condemns all the presumption toward God of the pseudo saints, who want to do and merit enough to reconcile God and to make Him their friend. For what else is this but to presume that they do the choosing[?] (LW 24:258).

Opening Prayer

L: Jesus said, "You did not choose Me, but I chose you." (John 15:16)

P: Blessed is the one You choose,[O Lord,] and bring near, to dwell in Your courts! (Psalm 65:4)

L: Now in Christ Jesus you who once were far off have been brought near

P: To Himself by the blood of Christ! (Ephesians 2:13–14)

L: Open our eyes, O Lord, that we may behold wondrous things out of Your Word.

P: Amen!

Sweet Freedom

Have participants work in pairs or small groups to complete each of the following sections. Review their discoveries with the whole group.

Because of the Arminian emphasis on the freedom of the human will, God's act of making you His child is regarded as a result of your personal decision. Stated another way, God will make you His child if you want Him to.

Discuss: *Does a baby personally decide he or she wants to be born, and then afterward, the baby's parents subsequently decide to conceive? In what way might the physical conception and birth of a child provide a helpful analogy for the way God chooses to make us His children? Use John 1:12–13 to help guide your discussion.* (The point of the analogy is that in birth, the baby is completely passive. He makes no decisions, but is acted upon. In the same way, no one becomes a child of God though his or her own decision.)

Arminians point to the words "to all who . . . believed in His name" (John 1:12), and say that this is good proof of freedom of the will. That is to say, you have to believe before God makes you His child. Yet, according to the following verses, where does faith come from?

Romans 10:17—Believing (faith) is given to you by the power of God's Word.

Ephesians 2:8–9—Faith is a gift of God.

2 Peter 1:1—Faith is something that is received or obtained from the outside, not something you conjure up in your own heart.

Arminians will also point to Romans 10:9 and say that you must first confess faith before you can be saved. But according to verse 8, where does your confession come from? From whence does this Word come according to verses 14–17? (When someone confesses faith in Christ, this confession comes about as a result of God's miraculous action in His Word, which is "near you," and which God has placed "in your mouth" by speaking it into your ears. This Word comes from the preaching of those whom God has sent.)

Discuss: *In what way might the Arminian teaching that God responds to you—rather than that God acts first—tempt you to doubt your forgiveness and salvation? Use Hebrews 12:1–2 to help guide your discussion.* (This Arminian teaching calls upon you to look first to yourself, to your own decision-making powers, and to your own personal commitment rather than to Jesus, "the author and perfecter of our faith" [NIV]. If God responds to you, how can you be certain that you have given Him enough reason to respond?)

Bells

The Salvation Army is best known for its red kettles for collecting coins at Christmas.

Discuss: *Do you personally contribute to the Salvation Army's collections? Why or why not?* (Answers may vary. Many participants have probably made contributions, especially as part of the generous feelings people experience during the holidays. Others may never have contributed for various reasons.)

Discuss: *Is there any distinction to be made between supporting the teaching efforts of another Christian church body and supporting that body's human care efforts? Why might such a distinction even matter? What cautions might be exercised in this regard?* (Some Lutherans follow the principle "Cooperation in externals." This means that it makes good sense to work together with other church bodies when attending to the physical needs of the community, as often happens in a local ministerial alliance. However, Lutherans might want to hesitate before contributing to another church body's teaching efforts. Why would you want to financially support what you believe to be false teachings?)

Discuss: *What would be a good relationship for a Lutheran congregation to have with its local ministerial alliance or food pantry? What about such things as World Day of Prayer or Meet Me at the Pole? Use the following Bible verses to guide your discussion.* (Many Lutheran congregations enthusiastically support ministerial alliance funds or food pantries. Participation in World Day of Prayer events or Meet Me at the Pole might put you in a situation in which you do not feel comfortable with the content of the prayers or teachings because they are contrary to God's Word, the Bible.)

Mark 8:15—Jesus warned that false teachings are like leaven, or yeast. They take root in the mind and expand, as yeast does in bread. This is why He warns, "Beware!"

Romans 16:17; 1 Timothy 4:6—Those who teach differently than God's Word teaches must be avoided so that they will not divert you from "the good doctrine that you have followed."

1 Corinthians 13:4–7—Love patiently forbears and tolerates, even though it does not allow itself to be knocked over by falsehoods.

2 Corinthians 8:19–21—Acts of generosity toward others are "for the glory of the Lord Himself and to show our good will."

1 Thessalonians 5:22—"Abstain from every form of evil."

Closing Prayer

Heavenly Father, grant Your mercy and grace to Your people in their many and various callings. Give them patience, and strengthen them in their Christian vocation of witness to the world and of service to their neighbor in Christ's name; through Jesus Christ, our Lord. Amen. (*LSB*, p. 311)

8 Salvation Army

A Message from Martin Luther

Christ Himself explains how He wants the words "No longer do I call you servants, but I call you My friends" to be understood. He says: "This friendship—the fact that I call you My friends—you do not have from yourselves; you have it because I chose you as friends through My suffering and death. . . ." This blasts and condemns all the presumption toward God of the pseudo saints, who want to do and merit enough to reconcile God and to make Him their friend. For what else is this but to presume that they do the choosing[?] (LW 24:258)

Opening Prayer

L: Jesus said, "You did not choose Me, but I chose you." (John 15:16)

P: Blessed is the one You choose, [O Lord,] and bring near, to dwell in Your courts! (Psalm 65:4)

L: Now in Christ Jesus you who once were far off have been brought near

P: To Himself by the blood of Christ! (Ephesians 2:13–14)

L: Open our eyes, O Lord, that we may behold wondrous things out of Your Word.

P: Amen!

Sweet Freedom

Does a baby personally decide he or she wants to be born, and then afterward, the baby's parents subsequently decide to conceive? In what way might the physical conception and birth of a child provide a helpful analogy for the way God chooses to make us His children? Use John 1:12–13 to help guide your discussion.

Arminians point the words "to all who . . . believed in His name" (John 1:12), and say that this is good proof of freedom of the will. That is to say, you have to believe before God makes

you His child. Yet, according to the following verses, where does faith come from?

Romans 10:17

Ephesians 2:8–9

2 Peter 1:1

Arminians will also point to Romans 10:9 and say that you must first confess faith before you can be saved. But according to verse 8, where does your confession come from? From whence does this Word come according to verses 14–17?

In what way might the Arminian teaching that God responds to you—rather than that God acts first—tempt you to doubt your forgiveness and salvation? Use Hebrews 12:1–2 to help guide your discussion.

Bells

Do you personally contribute to the Salvation Army's collections? Why or why not?

Is there any distinction to be made between supporting the teaching efforts of another Christian church body and supporting that body's human care efforts? Why might such a distinction even matter? What cautions might be exercised in this regard?

What would be a good relationship for a Lutheran congregation to have with its local ministerial alliance or food pantry? What about such things as World Day of Prayer or Meet Me at the Pole? Use the following Bible verses to guide your discussion.

Mark 8:15

Romans 16:17; 1 Timothy 4:6

1 Corinthians 13:4–7

2 Corinthians 8:19–21

1 Thessalonians 5:22

Participant Page 8 *One Christ, Many Creeds* copyright © 2008 Concordia Publishing House. Scripture: ESV® All rights reserved. Luther's Works, American Edition: vol. 24 copyright © 1961 Concordia Publishing House. All rights reserved. Reproduced by permission.

9

Church of the Nazarene

Lesson Focus

In Christ, we have a sure salvation; eternal life with Him is certain. In this session, we focus primarily on the Arminian teaching that Christ died potentially for everyone, so long as you decide to accept Him. This teaching, like the Arminian teachings in the previous two sessions, likewise teaches you to trust in yourself to some degree rather than to trust exclusively in your Lord Jesus Christ's death and resurrection.

Historical Context

Like the Salvation Army, the Church of the Nazarene is also a daughter of Methodism. Its main doctrinal emphases lie in personal holiness and sanctification. In a manner more pointed than is likely to be found in today's Methodism, the Church of the Nazarene teaches that Christians are able to reach a state of personal perfection in this life if the proper time and attention are given to the task. For this reason, the Church of the Nazarene is often referred to as a "Holiness church" or "Perfectionist church."

While its basic teachings have been promoted among Christians since the days of John Wesley, the Church of the Nazarene is a relatively new church body. Unlike the Salvation Army, its sister from "Mother Methodism," this church body was born in the United States. It was formed in 1908 as the result of a merger between several Holiness church bodies in the United States, and it has since spread—through its missionary efforts rather than immigration—into many countries throughout the world. Although one of the founding church groups in the 1908 merger was the Association of Pentecostal Churches of America, the Church of the Nazarene has since distanced itself from claims to speaking in mystical tongues, which is a central teaching of many Pentecostal church bodies today.

Distribute copies of Participant Page 9 and begin by reviewing the Luther quote and the Opening Prayer. This is also an appropriate time to distribute copies of the selected Quick Comparison Chart.

A Message from Martin Luther

[Christ died] for the sins of the whole world. It is certain that you are a part of the world. Do not let your heart deceive you by saying: "The Lord died for Peter and Paul; He rendered satisfaction for them, not for me." Therefore let everyone who has sin be summoned here, for He was made the expiation for the sins of the whole world and bore the sins of the whole world. (LW 30:237)

© Shutterstock/Victorian Traditions

Opening Prayer

L: Behold, the Lamb of God

P: **Who takes away the sin of the world!**
   (John 1:29)

L: In Christ God was reconciling the world to Himself,

P: **Not counting their trespasses against them.** (2 Corinthians 5:19)

L: Open our eyes, O Lord, that we may behold wondrous things out of Your Word.

P: **Amen!**

Saved/Not Saved?

Work through the questions and suggested Scriptures with the whole group. Why are some people saved and others not? Part of Calvinism's answer to this question is its idea that some people are predestined to hell from eternity (limited atonement). Arminianism finds this Calvinistic idea to be intolerable. In keeping with its teaching of the freedom of the will, Arminianism claims that Christ died *potentially* for everyone, but that you have to allow Him to die for you.

In what way do these Bible verses speak against Arminianism's idea that Christ's death was only potentially for all people?

John 3:16–17—God gave His only Son because He loved the whole world, not those who first loved Him.

John 6:51—Jesus gave His flesh "for the life of the world."

1 Timothy 2:4—God desires all people to be saved.

1 John 2:2—Jesus is the sacrifice not only for our sins, but "for the sins of the whole world."

Discuss: *If Christ died for all people, does that necessarily mean that all people will receive the benefits of His sacrificial death?* (The benefits of Christ's death are for all people of all time, but are applied only to those who have God's miraculous gift of faith.)

In what way do the following verses distinguish between those who will receive the benefits of Christ's death and resurrection and those who will not?

Mark 16:16—Those who do not believe will be condemned.

John 3:16–18—Whoever believes in Jesus will not be condemned but will have eternal life.

2 Thessalonians 2:10–15—Those who refuse to believe are "perishing," while those who "love the truth" (that is, believe) will be saved.

Discuss: *If Christ did not die for all people of all time everywhere, but only potentially died for you, how could you ever be certain that He definitely died for you? As you seek assurances of your forgiveness and eternal life, where would you be required to look if Christ truly did not die for all without exception?* (If Christ only potentially died for you, and if your salvation relied on your personal commitment to Jesus or your invitation that He come into your heart, you would end up looking at yourself for assurances of your forgiveness and eternal life.)

Holiness

A major aspect of teaching in the Church of the Nazarene, and also among many other groups called "Holiness church bodies," is the idea that Christians can attain personal perfection in this life. Stated another way, your sanctification can so completely permeate your life that you can eventually stop sinning.

Discuss: *In what sense is it good and true to say that God's gift of faith leads to a change in your behavior? What might you say about people who call themselves Christians, but whose actions and words make it seem as though they are unbelievers?* (God's gift of faith certainly works certain changes in you, especially in your outward behavior. As an extreme example, think about the murderer who becomes a Christian. Certainly, this new saint would want to stop committing murders. If he does not stop doing such terrible things, people will not think he is truly a Christian.)

What do the following verses have to say about the relationship between faith in Jesus and your behavior?

Galatians 5:16–26—When the Holy Spirit enters into you through Baptism, He begins to produce good fruit within you. These fruits mark a change in your actions, your words, and in your thinking.

1 Corinthians 6:9–11—"Such were some of you. But you were washed, you were sanctified, you were justified in the name of the Lord Jesus Christ and by the Spirit of our God."

Ephesians 4:17–24—"You must no longer walk as the Gentiles do."

Discuss: *Can we stop sinning on our own? Use Matthew 5:22, 28, 44 to guide your discussion.* (Of course, the general consensus will be that none of us has accomplished perfection or stopped sinning. The passages from the Sermon on the Mount are intended to show that even if a person were to refrain from sinful actions and sinful words [a very good thing to do!], sinful thoughts are unavoidable. Who can control the direction of his or her mind every moment of every day?)

In what way do the following Bible verses help explain why it is impossible for a Christian to stop sinning in this life?

Romans 7:15–25—Paul felt that he was totally incapable of doing right and very good at doing wrong. He did not enjoy this struggle.

Galatians 5:16–17—The Spirit and the flesh, coexisting in each Christian, are in continuous combat with each other.

Discuss: *Why is it for your personal blessing and benefit that you cannot stop struggling with sin and become personally holy? Asked another way, how is it that your personal struggle with sin prevents you from placing your certainty and confidence in yourself rather than in Christ? Use 2 Corinthians 12:7–10 to guide your discussion.* (The moment you completely stop sinning is the moment you no longer need to trust and rely upon Jesus. Why should you look to Christ for forgiveness when your need for forgiveness has gone away? Paul's thorn in his flesh taught him—as every Christian likewise must learn—that God's grace is sufficient in all things.)

Closing Prayer

O God, by the patient endurance of Your only-begotten Son You beat down the pride of the old enemy. Help us to treasure rightly in our hearts what our Lord has borne for our sakes that, after His example, we may bear with patience those things that are adverse to us; through Jesus Christ, our Lord. Amen. (LSB, p. 312)

9 Church of the Nazarene

A Message from Martin Luther

[Christ died] for the sins of the whole world. It is certain that you are a part of the world. Do not let your heart deceive you by saying: "The Lord died for Peter and Paul; He rendered satisfaction for them, not for me." Therefore let everyone who has sin be summoned here, for He was made the expiation for the sins of the whole world and bore the sins of the whole world. (LW 30:237)

Opening Prayer

L: Behold, the Lamb of God

P: **Who takes away the sin of the world!**
(John 1:29)

L: In Christ God was reconciling the world to Himself,

P: **Not counting their trespasses against them.**
(2 Corinthians 5:19)

L: Open our eyes, O Lord, that we may behold wondrous things out of Your Word.

P: Amen!

Saved/Not Saved?

In what way do these Bible verses speak against Arminianism's idea that Christ's death was only potentially for all people?

John 3:16–17

John 6:51

1 Timothy 2:4

1 John 2:2

If Christ died for all people, does that necessarily mean that all people will receive the benefits of His sacrificial death?

In what way do the following verses distinguish between those who will receive the benefits of Christ's death and resurrection and those who will not?

Mark 16:16

John 3:16–18

2 Thessalonians 2:10–15

If Christ did not die for all people of all time everywhere, but only potentially died for you, how could you ever be certain that He definitely died for you? As you seek assurances of your forgiveness and eternal life, where would you be required to look if Christ truly did not die for all without exception?

Holiness

In what sense is it good and true to say that God's gift of faith leads to a change in your behavior? What might you say about people who call themselves Christians, but whose actions and words make it seem as though they are unbelievers?

What do the following verses have to say about the relationship between faith in Jesus and your behavior?

Galatians 5:16–26

1 Corinthians 6:9–11

Ephesians 4:17–24

Can we stop sinning on our own? Use **Matthew 5:22, 28, 44** to guide your discussion.

In what way do the following Bible verses help explain why it is impossible for a Christian to stop sinning in this life?

Romans 7:15–25

Galatians 5:16–17

Why is it for your personal blessing and benefit that you cannot stop struggling with sin and become personally holy? Asked another way, how is it that your personal struggle with sin prevents you from placing your certainty and confidence in yourself rather than in Christ? Use **2 Corinthians 12:7–10** to guide your discussion.

Unit IV
Anabaptist Church Bodies

Baptists
Mennonites
Seventh-day Adventists

General Introduction

Unlike the Arminians, the Calvinists, and the Lutherans, the Anabaptists do not follow the teachings of a particular individual. Rather, the Anabaptists are primarily the followers of an idea. The name *Anabaptist* means "against Baptism." The several different Anabaptist groups of the sixteenth century (and following) all have one teaching in common: they do not baptize infants.

The refusal to baptize infants has at its core a specific understanding about Baptism (and for that matter, the Lord's Supper) that makes Anabaptists different from most other Christians. Anabaptists do not baptize babies because they believe Baptism is a human act rather than a divine miracle. (Similarly, they believe the Lord's Supper is a human act rather than a divine miracle.) Because infants cannot personally accept Jesus as Lord and confess the faith, the Anabaptists reason, no infant should ever be baptized. According to Anabaptist thinking, a person should only be baptized when he or she finally accepts God's will and makes a commitment to be a Christian.

Resistance to infant Baptism fits hand in glove with another central idea among Anabaptists that, for lack of a better term, might be called "anticreedalism." That is to say, Anabaptists feel a general aversion to any sort of creed or unifying statement of belief. While a particular Anabaptist might not have any argument with what is confessed in the Apostles', Nicene, or Athanasian Creed, that person would not want to be bound to any of the creeds because the creeds themselves are not spelled out in the Bible. A popular Anabaptist slogan is "No creeds but Christ."

While there are many different Anabaptist groups, each with its own history, three main groups stand out as significant for this study: the Baptists (an ironic name for those who take exception to infant Baptism), the Mennonites (followers of Menno Simons), and the Seventh-day Adventists (a group that highlights millennialism, another popular teaching accepted by many Anabaptists).

10

Baptists

Lesson Focus

In Christ, we have a sure salvation; eternal life with Him is certain. In this session, we focus primarily on the Anabaptist teaching that infants should not be baptized. This teaching robs you of certainty by calling upon you to "make your decision" or "personal commitment" in order to be called God's child through Baptism.

Historical Context

The keynote of Baptist theology is the freedom of individual belief. That is to say, the most important ideal for Baptists is that individual Christians have the right and ability to choose what they believe. This focus on the individual has led to a general dislike for creedal statements among Baptists. It is not that a Baptist would necessarily disagree with the Apostles' or the Nicene Creed; it is just that Baptists insist so strongly on the personal freedom of belief that they see no need for a creed that speaks the unity of the faith. This focus has led to another, perhaps surprising result: some Baptists are strongly Calvinistic (session 2), while others hold the totally opposite position of Arminianism (session 3). If there are common threads of teaching that hold all Baptists together, they would be (a) the refusal to baptize infants and (b) the view that Baptism and the Lord's Supper are not God's miraculous actions for us, but our actions of love and obedience toward God.

While the specific history of the Baptists is disputed by scholars, many believe that the main Baptist groups as we know them today trace their history to late sixteenth-century and early seventeenth-century England. These earliest Baptists separated themselves from the Church of England for a number of reasons, not the least of which was the rejection of infant Baptism. This separation, along with

© iStockphoto/mamado

the persecution and emigration that followed, led to the establishment of Baptist congregations in America.

Distribute copies of Participant Page 10 and the selected Quick Comparison Chart. Begin by reviewing the message from the Confessions and speaking together the Opening Prayer.

A Message from the Lutheran Confessions

Concerning Baptism, our churches teach that Baptism is necessary for salvation [Mark 16:16] and that God's grace is offered through Baptism [Titus 3:4–7]. They teach that children are to be baptized [Acts 2:38–39]. Being offered to God through Baptism, they are received into God's grace. (AC IX 1)

Opening Prayer

L: [Jesus said], "Let the children come to Me; do not hinder them,

P: "For to such belongs the kingdom of God." (Mark 10:14)

L: "Repent and be baptized every one of you in the name of Jesus Christ for the forgiveness of your sins,

P: "And you will receive the gift of the Holy Spirit. For the promise is for you and for your children." (Acts 2:38–39)

L: Open our eyes, O Lord, that we may behold wondrous things out of Your Word.

P: Amen!

Baptist Basics

Guide the whole group through the questions and suggested readings in this section. The most basic Anabaptist teaching about Baptism is that it is *not* a miracle God performs for you, but a powerless human act you perform for God.

In what way do the following Bible verses show that Baptism is God's powerful act and not merely a human act of obedience?

John 3:1–5—Jesus states, "You must be born again." These same words also may be translated from the Greek with equal faithfulness, "You must be born from above." This verse declares that the birth of water and the Spirit (Baptism) is something done from above (by God).

Titus 3:4–7—Baptism is the Holy Spirit's act of washing you with new birth and regenerating you.

1 Peter 3:21–22—"Baptism . . . now saves you." Who saves you? God does. How does He do it? Through Baptism!

Discuss: *Do these verses mean to suggest that there is no human activity at all in Baptism?* (Of course there is human activity. Mother and father bring the infant child, the pastor applies water in the name of God, and so on. In the case of adults, they voluntarily consent to Baptism after first being instructed in the Word of God. Yet all of these human activities simply cover the fact that God is the primary actor in Baptism, adopting, grafting, cleansing, regenerating, and filling the newly baptized with His Holy Spirit.)

How do the following Bible verses give you reason to think that even newborn infants should be baptized?

Matthew 28:19–20—Even infants are included in the words "all nations."

Luke 18:15–17—Jesus does not want *any* children barred from coming to Him.

Acts 2:38–39—God's promise given through Baptism "is for you and for your children."

Is Baptism an act of magic that you can receive in infancy and then forget about for the rest of your life? Stated another way, is it possible to miss out on the benefits God gave to you in your Baptism? (Many Anabaptists criticize the Lutheran theology and practice of infant Baptism, suggesting that Lutherans believe that a child can be baptized, then never be raised in God's Word and faith, and still live eternally with God in heaven.

While we certainly believe, in accordance with God's Word, that infants and all others are saved by means of Baptism, we would never conclude that Baptism is a magical act. It is better to think of Baptism as God's act of giving you His name, adopting you to be His own child [compare the "born from above" language in John 3:1–5 with Galatians 4:5–6]. Stated another way, in Baptism, God gives you His name and makes you His heir. Certainly you could walk away from your Baptism and pretend you were never adopted. However, to do so is to lose out on your inheritance! But when you remain a faithful child of God's house, loving your Father in response to His love for you, His promised inheritance will not fail to be yours.)

Discuss: *What certainties and assurances do Anabaptists and others lose when they refuse to believe in the divine power of Baptism?* (Rather than looking at the divine gift of Baptism as a reason to be certain they are saved, Anabaptists look at Baptism as something they must decide to do. They think of Baptism as an expression of their personal commitment to God. But this only teaches you to trust in yourself and in your commitment, rather than God. But what if your commitment should falter, or if you should begin to doubt whether you truly were serious when you made your decision? Baptism offers you no comforts of salvation and certainty of forgiveness unless faith regards it as God's act for you.)

Childlike Faith

The Anabaptist refusal to baptize infants rests on the assumption that infants do not have the ability to believe. Therefore, a child must wait until he or she is old enough to decide or make a commitment to Christ.

Discuss: *Is faith something you give to God or something God gives to you? The following Bible verses may be helpful to the discussion: Romans 10:17; Ephesians 2:1, 8–9.* (Contrary to Anabaptist belief, faith is a gift God miraculously gives to you through the life-giving power of His Word. Faith is "a gift of God" [Ephesians 2:8]. Without this divine gift of faith, we are dead in trespasses and sins—and dead men do nothing; they don't even believe!)

What do the following Bible verses say about infant faith?

Luke 1:15—John the Baptist, a human being like every other human being, heard the Word of God, and through the Word, had the Holy Spirit living in him from birth.

Luke 1:39–45—While still in his mother's womb, John leaped for joy when he heard the Virgin Mary's voice, whose speaking indicated that John's unborn Lord Jesus was near.

Matthew 18:6—Jesus speaks about "these little ones who believe in Me." The Greek word used here for "little" is *micro*, a word meaning "very small." You could translate Jesus' words as "these teeny, tiny believers."

Discuss: *Based on the Bible verses you studied in this section, is there really any difference between an infant who believes and a ninety-year-old who believes?* (Because faith is a miracle God performs through His Word, the idea that a ninety-year-old might believe is as surprising as the idea that an infant might believe. In each case, faith is worked through the miraculous power of the Word.)

Closing Prayer

Merciful Father, through Holy Baptism You called us to be Your own possession. Grant that our lives may evidence the working of Your Holy Spirit in love, joy, peace, patience, kindness, goodness, faithfulness, gentleness, and self-control, according to the image of Your only-begotten Son, Jesus Christ, our Savior. Amen. (*LSB*, p. 310)

10 Baptists

A Message from the Lutheran Confessions

Concerning Baptism, our churches teach that Baptism is necessary for salvation [Mark 16:16] and that God's grace is offered through Baptism [Titus 3:4–7]. They teach that children are to be baptized [Acts 2:38–39]. Being offered to God through Baptism, they are received into God's grace. (AC IX 1)

Opening Prayer

L: [Jesus said], "Let the children come to Me; do not hinder them,

P: **"For to such belongs the kingdom of God."**
(Mark 10:14)

L: "Repent and be baptized every one of you in the name of Jesus Christ for the forgiveness of your sins,

P: **"And you will receive the gift of the Holy Spirit. For the promise is for you and for your children."** (Acts 2:38–39)

L: Open our eyes, O Lord, that we may behold wondrous things out of Your Word.

P: **Amen!**

Baptist Basics

In what way do the following Bible verses show that Baptism is God's powerful act and not merely a human act of obedience?

John 3:1–5
_____

Titus 3:4–7
_____

1 Peter 3:21–22
_____

Do these verses mean to suggest that there is no human activity at all in Baptism?

_____
_____
_____

How do the following Bible verses give you reason to think that even newborn infants should be baptized?

Matthew 28:19–20
_____

Luke 18:15–17
_____

Acts 2:38–39
_____

Is Baptism an act of magic that you can receive in infancy and then forget about for the rest of your life? Stated another way, is it possible to miss out on the benefits God gave to you in your Baptism?

_____

What certainties and assurances do Anabaptists and others lose when they refuse to believe in the divine power of Baptism?

_____

Childlike Faith

Is faith something you give to God or something God gives to you? The following Bible verses may be helpful to the discussion: **Romans 10:17; Ephesians 2:1, 8–9.**

_____

What do the following Bible verses say about infant faith?

Luke 1:15
_____

Luke 1:39–45
_____

Matthew 18:6
_____

Based on the Bible verses you studied in this section, is there really any difference between an infant who believes and a ninety-year-old who believes?

_____
_____

Participant Page **10** *One Christ, Many Creeds* copyright © 2008 Concordia Publishing House. Scripture: ESV® *Concordia: The Lutheran Confessions*, second edition, copyright © 2006 Concordia Publishing House. All rights reserved. Reproduced by permission.

11

Mennonites

Lesson Focus

In Christ, we have a sure salvation; eternal life with Him is certain. In this session, we focus primarily on the Anabaptist teachings that (a) immersion must be practiced in Baptism and (b) the Lord's Supper is not something God does for you, but something you do for God. Because, according to Anabaptist thinking, there are many other things that can be done for God, the Lord's Supper is a low priority. This is illustrated by the historic Mennonite practice of celebrating the Lord's Supper only twice a year, but having many large and well-developed programs of mutual aid and worldwide relief efforts. This may sound like a trivial distinction; however, in the end, this teaching of the Mennonites and other Anabaptists calls on you to find certainty in your own works rather than in the gifts and works of God.

Historical Context

The founder of the Mennonites was Menno Simons (ca. 1492–ca. 1559), a Roman Catholic priest who converted to Anabaptist theology and was "rebaptized." Simons planted so many Anabaptist congregations that his name eventually became associated with the whole group. Like the Baptists, the Mennonites do not believe in the practice of infant Baptism or in the divine power of Baptism and the Lord's Supper. Like the Pentecostals, the Mennonites believe in the inner guidance of the Holy Spirit, operating apart from the revealed Word of the Scriptures. This second motif of Mennonite teaching has led scholars to classify Mennonites as an "Inner Light" church body.

There are many "varieties" of Mennonites today, which can be distinguished by their actions and outward appearance. Many Mennonites reject the temptations of the modern world by not using motorized equipment or electricity and by wearing simple clothing most other people would regard as old-fashioned. Other Mennonites make full use of these things and dress in up-to-date clothing. Between these two extremes are many Mennonite groups that try to hang on to a little bit of both.

Distribute copies of Participant Page 11 and continue. You may also want to hand out copies of the Quick Comparison Chart at this time.

A Message from Martin Luther

In the Lord's Supper, Christ's body and blood are truly and actually present. They are truly administered with those things that are seen, bread and wine. And we speak of the presence of the living Christ, for we know that "death no longer has dominion over Him" (Romans 6:9). (AP X 57)

Opening Prayer

L: [Jesus said,] "This is My body. . . . This is My blood." (Mark 14:22, 24)

P: For as often as you eat this bread and drink this cup, you proclaim the Lord's death until He comes. (1 Corinthians 11:24–26)

L: The cup of blessing that we bless, is it not a participation in the blood of Christ?

P: The bread that we break, is it not a participation in the body of Christ? (1 Corinthians 10:16)

L: Open our eyes, O Lord, that we may behold wondrous things out of Your Word.

P: Amen!

Whose Work Is This?

Participants may work through this section individually or in small groups. Review with the whole group. Aside from the refusal to baptize infants (previous session), the second distinctive mark of Anabaptists is the insistence that Baptism be performed by immersion. (Menno Simons insisted on immersion, but some modern Mennonites have begun to depart from this tradition, allowing for Baptism by sprinkling.)

Discuss: *In what way does the Anabaptist teaching that Baptism is truly a human work make it crucial that Baptisms be performed in a certain way?* (If Baptism is indeed a human work, as the Anabaptists wrongly believe, then there would be great concern that the application of Baptism be exactly right. Stated another way, if Baptism is nothing more than a divine command to "do this," then Christians will want to be certain they "do this" in exactly the right way.)

Discuss: *In what way does the Bible's teaching that Baptism is a gift of God allow for more freedom in terms of the exact method used to apply water?* (The Bible teaches that Baptism is water to which God's Word of promise has been added. While the water is certainly essential, the main point of Baptism is God's Word of promise. For this reason, so long as Baptism includes both water and the Word [Matthew 28:19–20], the exact manner of applying the water to the person becomes secondary.)

What type of application of water seems to be indicated in the following verses about Baptism? (Both of these verses suggest that immersion is indeed a fine way of baptizing.)

Matthew 3:13–17—Jesus was immersed at His Baptism.

Acts 8:36–38—The Ethiopian eunuch also appears to have been immersed.

According to Mark 7:4, must Baptism (washing) always be performed by immersion? (The Greek word *baptizo* is also used here, but immersing does not seem practical for washing [baptizing] "dining couches." In this case, the word *baptizo* refers to sprinkling or pouring.)

Discuss: *What are the necessary parts of Baptism? Use Matthew 28:19–20 to help guide your discussion.* (This topic was addressed earlier. It is important to emphasize that the mode or application of water in Baptism is not the point. Rather, the Word of God's promise is the main point. When Anabaptists reject God's Word of promise in Baptism, they are left only with the mode or application on which to focus their attention.)

Empty Bread

In keeping with its Anabaptist tradition and this tradition's disbelief in the divine power of the Sacraments, Mennonites believe the Lord's Supper is a purely human work that Christians must perform in obedience to God.

Discuss: *What does the word* is *mean? This is important because the issue concerning the Lord's Supper boils down to one question: what does the word* is *mean when Jesus says, "This is My body. . . . This is My blood" (Matthew 26:26, 28)?* (In the end, the word *is* means "is," or "to be." The word does not mean "represents" or "symbolizes." There are Greek words that would much more easily convey these other meanings, if that is what Jesus had intended. Jesus deliberately used the word *is* when He said, "This is My body. . . . This is My blood.")

In what way do the following Bible verses help you understand that the bread and wine in the Lord's Supper are truly Jesus' body and blood, rather than symbols or representations of Jesus' body and blood?

1 Corinthians 10:16—If the Lord's Supper only symbolized or represented Christ's body and blood, we would have no participation, no fellowship, no *koinonia* with the body and blood of Christ when we eat the bread and drink the wine.

1 Corinthians 11:27, 29—In the same way, it would also be impossible to sin against the body and blood of Christ if His body and blood were not present in the Lord's Supper, where people might partake of it "in an unworthy manner."

Discuss: *What certainties and assurances do Anabaptists miss when they refuse to believe in the divine power of the Lord's Supper?* (As with Baptism, the Anabaptist's rejection of God's promises in the Lord's Supper leaves them only with the outward performance of the meal. No certainty or assurance of forgiveness of sins is given to those who look at this meal as merely something they do for God.)

Closing Prayer

Blessed Savior, Jesus Christ, You have given Yourself to us in [the] holy Sacrament. Keep us in Your faith and favor that we might live in You even as You live in us. May Your body and blood preserve us in the true faith to life everlasting. Hear us for the sake of Your name. Amen. (*LSB*, p. 308)

11 Mennonites

A Message from Martin Luther

In the Lord's Supper, Christ's body and blood are truly and actually present. They are truly administered with those things that are seen, bread and wine. And we speak of the presence of the living Christ, for we know that "death no longer has dominion over Him" (Romans 6:9). (AP X 57)

Opening Prayer

L: [Jesus said,] "This is My body. . . . This is My blood." (Mark 14:22, 24)

P: For as often as you eat this bread and drink this cup, you proclaim the Lord's death until He comes. (1 Corinthians 11:24–26)

L: The cup of blessing that we bless, is it not a participation in the blood of Christ?

P: The bread that we break, is it not a participation in the body of Christ? (1 Corinthians 10:16)

L: Open our eyes, O Lord, that we may behold wondrous things out of Your Word.

P: Amen!

Whose Work Is This?

In what way does the Anabaptist teaching that Baptism is truly a human work make it crucial that Baptisms be performed in a certain way?

_____

_____

In what way does the Bible's teaching that Baptism is a gift of God allow for more freedom in terms of the exact method used to apply water?

_____

_____

What type of application of water seems to be indicated in the following verses about Baptism?

Matthew 3:13–17
_____

Acts 8:36–38
_____

According to **Mark 7:4**, must Baptism (washing) always be performed by immersion?

_____

_____

What are the necessary parts of Baptism? Use **Matthew 28:19–20** to help guide your discussion.

_____

Empty Bread

What does the word _is_ mean? This is important because the issue concerning the Lord's Supper boils down to one question: what does the word _is_ mean when Jesus says, "This is My body. . . . This is My blood" (**Matthew 26:26, 28**)?

_____

_____

In what way do the following Bible verses help you understand that the bread and wine in the Lord's Supper are truly Jesus' body and blood, rather than symbols or representations of Jesus' body and blood?

1 Corinthians 10:16
_____

1 Corinthians 11:27, 29
_____

What certainties and assurances do Anabaptists miss when they refuse to believe in the divine power of the Lord's Supper?

_____

_____

Participant Page 11 _One Christ, Many Creeds_ copyright © 2008 Concordia Publishing House. Scripture: ESV® _Concordia: The Lutheran Confessions_, second edition, copyright © 2006 Concordia Publishing House. All rights reserved. Reproduced by permission.

12

Seventh-day Adventists

Lesson Focus

In Christ, we have a sure salvation; eternal life with Him is certain. In this session, we focus primarily on the Seventh-day Adventist teaching that certain laws and ceremonies of the Old Testament—the Sabbath observance in particular—must be maintained. This teaching leads you to find certainty based on what you do rather than trusting exclusively in your Lord Jesus Christ's death and resurrection for you.

Historical Context

The Seventh-day Adventists are part of a larger religious movement called Adventism, which places a high emphasis on the return of Christ on the Last Day. While Adventism (also called Millennialism) has ancient roots (for example, the Montanists), most of today's Adventists are the products of a resurgence of Millennialism that took place during the nineteenth century.

The Seventh-day Adventists began to gather as a group in the 1840s, having broken away from their parent group of Adventists called the Millerites. The Millerites had become fractured and disillusioned after several predictions of Christ's return failed to come true. Having broken away from the Millerites, the Seventh-day Adventists followed teachings of Mrs. Ellen G. White, whose ecstatic visions claimed that the return of Christ was indeed imminent, and that Saturday, not Sunday, was the truly proper day for true believers to worship. Mrs. White also taught that the Antichrist had introduced the practice of worship on Sunday.

In addition to their millennialist and Sabbath beliefs, the Seventh-day Adventists also advocate the sanctification of the physical body by forbidding the use of tobacco and alcohol and by following rigorous dietary and exercise guidelines. Their view of the Sacraments is the same as that held by the other church bodies in this unit, and they believe in direct prophecy by the Holy Spirit, in a manner similar to that believed by the Pentecostals/Assemblies of God.

Distribute copies of Participant Page 12. Review the Message from Martin Luther and join in the Opening Prayer. If desired, also provide copies of the appropriate Quick Comparison Chart at this time.

A Message from Martin Luther

Pastors should not make an issue of the fact that one observes a holy day and another does not. Let each one peacefully keep to his custom. Only do not do away with all holy days. . . . Yet the people are to be taught that the only reason for keeping these festivals is to learn the Word of God. If one wishes to do manual labor, he may do so in his own way. For God requires observance

© Shutterstock/Mary Terriberry

of these church ordinances by us only on account of the teaching, as Paul says in Col. 2 [:16]: "Therefore let no one pass judgment on you in questions of food and drink or with regard to a festival or new moon or sabbath." (LW 40:298)

Opening Prayer

L: Let no one pass judgment on you in questions of food and drink,

P: Or with regard to a festival or a new moon or a Sabbath.

L: These are a shadow of the things to come,

P: But the substance belongs to Christ.

(Colossians 2:16–17)

L: Open our eyes, O Lord, that we may behold wondrous things out of Your Word.

P: Amen!

Saturday Sabbath

Review the questions and Scripture verses in these two sections with the whole group. The most important day-to-day teaching of the Seventh-day Adventists is that Saturday (the Jewish Sabbath) is the only proper day for Christians to worship. This explains the "Seventh-day" part of this church body's name.

According to Colossians 2:16–17, in what way do New Testament Christians regard the observance of the Sabbath? (Along with the other features of Old Testament worship [sacrifices, ceremonies, special festivals], the Sabbath observance was "a shadow of the things to come," namely, Christ.)

Read Hebrews 10:1–10. Compare the phrase "shadow of the things to come" (Colossians 2:17) to the similar phrase in Hebrews 10:1. In particular, what does verse 9 have to say about what Christ has done with the laws of the Old Testament, including the Sabbath law? ("Shadow of the things to come" refers to the first coming of our Lord Jesus Christ, whose death and resurrection fulfilled every aspect of Old Testament worship. By His death and resurrection, Christ fulfilled every law and demand of the Old Testament. For this reason, just as Christians no longer offer blood

sacrifices because Christ is the last sacrifice, so also they are no longer bound by the rules and regulations of Old Testament worship. To insist that Old Testament worship laws still be observed is to deny Christ's all-encompassing work of salvation.)

Discuss: *Do these verses mean that it is no longer important for Christians to "Remember the Sabbath Day, to keep it holy" (Exodus 20:8)?* (Christ has fulfilled all of God's laws for us, and thus we are no longer under any obligation to observe them. Stated another way, we are saved by grace through faith in Christ Jesus, not by observing the Law. Why do we keep the Ten Commandments today? These commandments show us how to love God and our neighbor. Love, not obligation, compels Christians to faithfully gather for worship. For further help in this matter, read Romans 13:8–10 and Galatians 5:14.)

What do the following verses say about the importance of Christian worship?

Acts 2:42—Worship consists of devoting oneself "to the apostles' teaching [that is, hearing God's life-giving Word] and fellowship, to the breaking of bread [that is, the Lord's Supper] and the prayers."

Romans 14:5–6—Worship no longer consists of the obligation to observe a certain day.

Hebrews 10:25—Worship is not only God's way of providing you with His benefits (Acts 2:42), but it is also a way of caring for the whole body of Christ by "not neglecting to meet together."

Discuss: *How might the Seventh-day Adventist emphasis on Saturday worship tempt people to look at themselves for certainty of their salvation, rather than looking solely to Christ? It may be helpful to use Galatians 4:10–11 in the discussion.* (The Galatians, like the Seventh-day Adventists, fell into the trap of thinking that in order to be saved, Christians must fulfill certain obligations in addition to believing in Jesus. Stated another way, like the Galatians, Seventh-day Adventists believe that you have to adopt certain Jewish practices in order to be saved. Paul calls this a return to slavery.)

What do Luke 24:1–2 and Acts 20:7 suggest about why many Christian congregations might schedule worship mainly on Sunday rather than Saturday? (Both of these verses speak about Christ's resurrection from the dead on the first day of the week [Sunday], a good day to gather in worship to receive the benefits of Christ's death and resurrection.)

Thousands

The "Adventist" part of this church body's name has to do with its millennialist beliefs, which claim that Jesus will establish a physical kingdom here on earth and reign over it for a thousand years of peace and prosperity before the Last Day.

The idea of Christ's thousand-year reign over a physical kingdom here on earth comes from a literal reading of Revelation 20:1–7. According to 14:1–3, is it a good idea to take all the numbers in the Book of Revelation as literal rather than symbolic? (If every number in Revelation were taken literally, we would all be lost! Revelation 14:1–3 speaks about 144,000 people being saved, a number that would surely have been fulfilled long before now.)

What does John 18:36 say about a supposed physical reign of Christ in a kingdom established here on earth? (Because Jesus declared, "My kingdom is not of this world," we can be sure that the idea of millennialism is purely a human fabrication. Millennialism works directly against the clear words of Jesus.)

Millennialism/Adventism is famous for its predictions about when Christ will return to set up His supposed physical kingdom. How does Mark 13:31–32 show that such predictions are impossible to make? (Jesus declared, "Concerning that day or that hour, no one knows, not even the angels in heaven, nor the Son [in the weakness of His humiliation], but only the Father." These clear words make it certain that all predictions of our Lord's return can only be lies and should therefore not be trusted in the least.)

Discuss: *In what way might millennialism/Adventism teach you to have confidence in something other than Christ for your salvation? Is such confidence really any sort of confidence at all?* (Millennialism teaches you to focus your attentions more on "End Times Fever," if you will, than on the Christ who loves, guards, and cares for you every moment of every day. Millennialists pin their hopes not on the words of the Scriptures, but on so-called secret knowledge. These hopes, which do not come from God, cannot help but disappoint, mislead, and perhaps even destroy faith.)

Closing Prayer

Lord Jesus Christ, giver and perfecter of our faith, we thank and praise You for continuing among us the preaching of Your Gospel for our instruction and edification. Send Your blessing upon the Word, which has been spoken to us, and by Your Holy Spirit increase our saving knowledge of You, that day by day we may be strengthened in the divine truth and remain steadfast in Your grace. Give us strength to fight the good fight and by faith to overcome all the temptations of Satan, the flesh, and the world so that we may finally receive the salvation of our souls; for You live and reign with the Father and the Holy Spirit, one God, now and forever. Amen. (*LSB*, p. 308)

12 Seventh-day Adventists

A Message from Martin Luther

Pastors should not make an issue of the fact that one observes a holy day and another does not. Let each one peacefully keep to his custom. Only do not do away with all holy days. . . . Yet the people are to be taught that the only reason for keeping these festivals is to learn the Word of God. If one wishes to do manual labor, he may do so in his own way. For God requires observance of these church ordinances by us only on account of the teaching, as Paul says in Col. 2 [:16]: "Therefore let no one pass judgment on you in questions of food and drink or with regard to a festival or new moon or sabbath." (*LW* 40:298)

Opening Prayer

L: Let no one pass judgment on you in questions of food and drink,

P: Or with regard to a festival or a new moon or a Sabbath.

L: These are a shadow of the things to come,

P: But the substance belongs to Christ.

(Colossians 2:16–17)

L: Open our eyes, O Lord, that we may behold wondrous things out of Your Word.

P: Amen!

Saturday Sabbath

According to **Colossians 2:16–17**, in what way do New Testament Christians regard the observance of the Sabbath?

_____

Read Hebrews 10:1–10. Compare the phrase "shadow of the things to come" (**Colossians 2:17**) to the similar phrase in **Hebrews 10:1**. In particular, what does **verse 9** have to say about what Christ has done with the laws of the Old Testament, including the Sabbath law?

_____

Do these verses mean that it is no longer important for Christians to "Remember the Sabbath Day, to keep it holy" (**Exodus 20:8**)?

_____

What do the following verses say about the importance of Christian worship?

Acts 2:42

_____

Romans 14:5–6

_____

Hebrews 10:25

_____

How might the Seventh-day Adventist emphasis on Saturday worship tempt people to look at themselves for certainty of their salvation, rather than looking solely to Christ? It may be helpful to use **Galatians 4:10–11** in the discussion.

_____

What do **Luke 24:1–2** and **Acts 20:7** suggest about why many Christians congregations might schedule worship mainly on Sunday rather than Saturday?

Thousands

The idea of Christ's thousand-year reign over a physical kingdom here on earth comes from a literal reading of **Revelation 20:1–7**. According to **14:1–3**, is it a good idea to take all the numbers in the Book of Revelation as literal rather than symbolic?

_____

What does **John 18:36** say about a supposed physical reign of Christ in a kingdom established here on earth?

_____

Millennialism/Adventism is famous for its predictions about when Christ will return to set up His supposed physical kingdom. How does **Mark 13:31–32** show that such predictions are impossible to make?

_____

In what way might millennialism/Adventism teach you to have confidence in something other than Christ for your salvation? Is such confidence really any sort of confidence at all?

_____

Participant Page 12 *One Christ, Many Creeds* copyright © 2008 Concordia Publishing House. Scripture: ESV® Luther's Works, American Edition: vol. 40 copyright © 1958 Fortress Press. Used by permission. All rights reserved. Reproduced by permission.

Unit V
Late Arrivals

United Church of Christ
Evangelical Lutheran Church in America
Pentecostalism/Assemblies of God
Emerging Churches

General Introduction

Just as some church bodies form as a result of schism (such as the Great Schism of 1054), others form as a result of union. Among the many union church bodies, which combine the teachings of two or more separate groups, the United Church of Christ stands out as a prime example. This church body has the word *united* in its name, which hints at the theological combinations that have taken place. Other combinations are not so easily detected. For example, the name *Evangelical Lutheran Church in America* gives no indication that this church body has incorporated many non-Lutheran teachings in its midst. Both of these church bodies are included in this unit called "Late Arrivals" not only because they were formed relatively recently (in comparison to the others) but also because some of their teachings are unprecedented in the history of the Christian Church.

Another late arrival is the phenomenon frequently called Pentecostalism, which has led to the formation of many congregations and church bodies. Prominent among these is the Assemblies of God. Chief among the attributes of Pentecostalism/Assemblies of God are claims that God the Holy Spirit speaks directly to individuals, apart from the Scriptures, and that Christians will manifest the indwelling of the Holy Spirit by speaking in tongues or by displaying other supernatural gifts; there is a strong emphasis on emotional revivalism.

13
United Church of Christ

Lesson Focus

In Christ, we have a sure salvation; eternal life with Him is certain. In this session we focus primarily on the false idea that matters of the Christian religion are open to human opinions, and that you can believe what you want to believe and I will believe what I want to believe. This false teaching leads to great uncertainty because it leaves you to trust totally in yourself—especially your ability to form a good opinion—for your salvation.

Historical Context

The formal birth date for the United Church of Christ (UCC) is June 25, 1957, when the General Council of Congregational Christian Churches (organized 1931) and the Evangelical and Reformed Church (organized 1934) joined together as one church body. Although the UCC was born relatively recently, the mind-set that allowed for its creation actually extends back to September 27, 1817. On this date, Frederick William III of Germany announced the Prussian Union, which legally required the Reformed (Calvinist) and Lutheran Churches in Germany to join together as one church body. (Many Lutherans protested. Some of them left Germany and eventually formed Lutheran church bodies in the United States, including The Lutheran Church—Missouri Synod).

When people want to combine church bodies such as the Calvinists and the Lutherans, they do so with the assumption that differences in theology really do not matter all that much. (To the contrary, this Bible study builds on the assumption that differences in theology matter a great deal). In making statements concerning their beliefs, the UCC readily admits that they receive the historic creeds and confessions as testimonies, but not as tests of the faith (http://www.ucc.org/beliefs).

Distribute copies of Participant Page 13 and work through the opening materials. You may also want to hand out copies of the Quick Comparison Chart at this time.

A Message from Martin Luther

"Away with human opinions!" (LW 27:31).

Opening Prayer

L: Trust in the LORD with all your heart,

P: And do not lean on your own understanding. (Proverbs 3:5)

L: Sanctify them in the truth;

P: Your Word is truth! (John 17:17)

L: Open our eyes, O Lord, that we may behold wondrous things out of Your Word.

P: Amen!

Free to Choose

The UCC faith states, "We seek a balance between freedom of conscience and accountability to the apostolic faith" (www.ucc.org/beliefs).

Discuss: *What important assumptions does this UCC statement make concerning the individual's ability to exercise "freedom of conscience"?* (At the heart of the matter is the assumption that "freedom of conscience" is, by definition, good, because the conscience itself is naturally good and able to please God.)

Discuss: *When Luther was told to turn away from the biblical teachings that he was publishing in the Church and to publish such things no more, he refused. Luther stated, "My conscience is held captive by the Word of God." What did Luther mean by this?* (Note: These words are part of Luther's well-known "Here I Stand" speech delivered at the conclusion of the Diet of Worms. Luther did not concern himself in the least with freedom of conscience. His conscience was a captive, bound by the words of the Scriptures. When Luther's conscience felt guilty, he believed the Scriptures' word of forgiveness. By the power of God's Holy Spirit, Luther forced himself to remain faithful to the Word, even when his conscience was full of fear.)

What does Romans 2:14–15 have to say about the source of the conscience? (Contrary to the UCC statement, the conscience does not exist apart from God's Word, as if we should choose between the two, but rather, "the work of the law is written on their hearts.")

In what way do the following Bible passages speak about the so-called "freedom of conscience"?

Matthew 15:10–20—The human heart is not the source of good, but the source of every evil. Perhaps it should not be trusted!

Colossians 2:8—Human ideas and opinions (the source of the UCC's "freedom of conscience") are a source of deception and captivity to sin.

1 Timothy 6:20—Christians must "guard the deposit entrusted to [them]," rather than allowing themselves to swerve away into "irreverent babble and contradictions."

It's All Relative

Consider again the UCC statement: "The UCC therefore receives the historic creeds and confessions of our ancestors as testimonies, but not tests of the faith." Essentially, this statement from the UCC means "We will believe what we want to believe."

Discuss: *What is the value of being unified with other Christians in one confession of faith?* (By sharing a common confession of faith, peace and unity of the Spirit grow [Ephesians 4:1–6]. The false unity characterized by agreement to disagree or "freedom of conscience" leads to the unprofitable conclusion that it really does not matter what you personally believe.)

What do the following Bible passages have to say about the importance of avoiding those who teach something that they thought up for themselves rather than something they learned from God's Word, the Bible?

Romans 16:17–18—Christians must avoid those who "cause divisions" by teaching things that are contrary to God's Word. Such people "deceive the hearts of the naive."

2 Thessalonians 2:10b–12—Those who "refused to love the truth" fall into a strong delusion sent by God. This act of judgment makes it impossible for them to see that they are the victims of lies. Under this delusion, such people mistakenly believe they are Christian, even though they are far from the Word.

1 Timothy 1:3–5—The so-called "freedom of conscience," operating apart from the Word, leads only to speculations. Speculations give no profit at all to the faith.

Discuss: *In what way does the idea "We will believe what we want to believe" give you great protection? (See Acts 5:29.) On the other hand, in what way can this idea rob you of all certainty and confidence in believing?* (The idea of freedom of belief will give you great courage on those occasions when you might feel pressured to go along with a teaching that is not in keeping with God's Word, the Bible. The apostles themselves faced this difficulty. But rather than obeying the authorities, who insisted that the apostles stop preaching about Jesus, the apostles declared, "We must obey God rather than men" [Acts 5:29]. Essentially, the apostles said, "We will believe what we want to believe."

On the other side of the coin, this insistence on believing what you want to believe will lead you into great sin, despair, and even death if you should choose to believe what is contrary to the Scriptures! That is what makes the UCC statement so dangerous to faith and certainty of salvation.)

Closing Prayer

O holy and most merciful God, You have taught us the way of Your commandments. We implore You to pour out Your grace into our hearts. Cause it to bear fruit in us that, being ever mindful of Your mercies and Your laws, we may always be directed to Your will and daily increase in love toward You and one another. Enable us to resist all evil and to live a godly life. Help us to follow the example of our Lord and Savior, Jesus Christ, and to walk in His steps until we shall possess the kingdom that has been prepared for us in heaven; through Jesus Christ, our Lord. Amen. (*LSB*, p. 308)

13 United Church of Christ

A Message from Martin Luther

"Away with human opinions!" (LW 27:31)

Opening Prayer

L: Trust in the LORD with all your heart,

P: And do not lean on your own understanding. (Proverbs 3:5)

L: Sanctify them in the truth;

P: Your Word is truth! (John 17:17)

L: Open our eyes, O Lord, that we may behold wondrous things out of Your Word.

P: Amen!

Free to Choose

What important assumptions does this UCC statement make concerning the individual's ability to exercise "freedom of conscience"?

_____

_____

When Luther was told to turn away from the biblical teachings that he was publishing in the Church and to publish such things no more, he refused. Luther stated, "My conscience is held captive by the Word of God." What did Luther mean by this?

_____

_____

What does **Romans 2:14–15** have to say about the source of the conscience?

_____

_____

In what way do the following Bible passages speak about the so-called "freedom of conscience"?

Matthew 15:10–20
_____

Colossians 2:8
_____

1 Timothy 6:20
_____

It's All Relative

What is the value of being unified with other Christians in one confession of faith?

_____

_____

What do the following Bible passages have to say about the importance of avoiding those who teach something that they thought up for themselves rather than something they learned from God's Word, the Bible?

Romans 16:17–18
_____

2 Thessalonians 2:10b–12
_____

1 Timothy 1:3–5
_____

In what way does the idea "We will believe what we want to believe" give you great protection? (See **Acts 5:29.**) On the other hand, in what way can this idea rob you of all certainty and confidence in believing?

_____

_____

14

Evangelical Lutheran Church in America

Lesson Focus

In Christ, we have a sure salvation; eternal life with Him is certain. In this session, we focus primarily on the Evangelical Lutheran Church in America (ELCA) and its departure from the clear words of the Bible. Like the United Church of Christ, the ELCA's public position essentially boils down to the idea that you can believe what you want to believe about God and His Word, the Bible. The ELCA is not the only Lutheran church body worldwide that believes this. Rather, the ELCA is representative of a newer form of Lutheranism that has departed from the original, historic theology of the first Lutherans. It should also be noted that the same sort of theology found in the ELCA today is also found among many other church bodies, including Presbyterians, Methodists, and Anglicans/Episcopalians. Much of the content of this session applies also to these other bodies.

Historical Context

At its constituting convention, April 30–May 3, 1987, the Evangelical Lutheran Church in America (ELCA) formally united three Lutheran church bodies: the Association of Evangelical Lutheran Churches (AELC), the American Lutheran Church (ALC), and the Lutheran Church in America (LCA).

The ELCA is placed in the unit concerning "Late Arrivals" not merely because of the fairly recent date of its constituting convention, but also because of its "new" theology, which is quite distinct from the confessional theology of the historic Lutherans. This new theology includes, among other things, the assumption that the Bible *is not* the Word of God, but rather it *contains* the Word of God. This simple shift has allowed the ELCA, like many other "modern" or "liberal" church bodies, to develop doctrinal positions and church practices that are far removed from the teachings of Scripture.

Some of these far-removed teachings include (a) a "demythologized" view of the Scriptures, which states that certain parts of the Bible, such as the creation story and Jonah's three days in the belly of a fish, are only myths (this is built on the belief that not everything in the Bible is divine); (b) the theology and practice of women's ordination; and (c) the toleration and even acceptance of such things as abortion and homosexuality as an acceptable lifestyle.

Important note: Many individual Christians who are members of ELCA congregations might not believe any of these new teachings. However, it must be recognized that these are the positions of the ELCA leadership and many of their clergy, in spite of what the people in the pews might believe.

Distribute copies of Participant Page 14 and the Quick Comparison Chart. Begin with the Message from Martin Luther and the Opening Prayer.

A Message from Martin Luther

[God's Word] is called iron because of its inflexible and invincible straightness, or, as blessed Augustine has observed, its inflexible righteousness. For however many have tried to twist and bend the Word of God to their own interpretation, it has remained invincibly straight, convicting as liars those who have distorted it. . . . However, when some ascribe to the Scriptures the flexibility of a waxen nose and say that it is like a bending reed, this is due to the work of those who misuse the holy Word of God for their incompetent and unstable opinions. . . . They reach the point where the Word of God, which is fitting for everything, fits nothing. (LW 14:338)

Opening Prayer

L: No prophecy of Scripture comes from someone's own interpretation.

P: **For no prophecy was ever produced by the will of man,**

L: But men spoke from God.

P: **They spoke from God as they were carried along by the Holy Spirit.** (2 Peter 1:20–21)

L: Open our eyes, O Lord, that we may behold wondrous things out of Your Word.

P: **Amen!**

The Lutheran Difference

Review the remaining sections of the Participant Page with the whole group. There is one critical point for understanding the differences between the teachings of the ELCA (along with some other church bodies worldwide) and the teachings of historic Lutherans. This critical point can be put in the form of a question: *is the Bible God's Word, or does the Bible only* contain *God's Word?*

What phrase does the Nicene Creed use to describe the Bible? Why do you suppose a statement about the Bible was included in this creed? (The Nicene Creed states that the Holy Spirit "spoke by the prophets." With these words, Christians confess faith that the Bible is God speaking through the prophets. This phrase appears in the creed because, in part, it is an article of the faith to say that the Bible is God's Word. There is no way to prove it, just as there is no way to prove that God created in six days or that Christ rose from the dead. The only reason that Christians believe the Bible is God's Word is on account of the Bible's own testimony about itself.)

What do the following passages from the Bible have to say about the Bible? (These passages show that the Bible regards itself as God's Word, not merely as containing God's Word.)

2 Timothy 3:16—"All Scripture is breathed out by God," that is, given by God. (Note: This verse refers, in the first instance, to the Old Testament Scriptures.)

2 Peter 1:20–21—No Scripture came from a merely human source, but all came about as its human scribes "were carried along by the Holy Spirit."

2 Peter 3:15–16—Peter identifies Paul's letters (what later became the bulk of the New Testament) as Scriptures.

Revelation 22:18–19—John, the last writer of the New Testament, speaks a warning of condemnation to anyone who would add or subtract to this book. The belief that the Bible only contains the Word of God is nothing other than a subtraction from the book.

Discuss: *Why might it seem attractive to say that the Bible only* contains *God's Word, rather than that the Bible* is *God's Word?* (By saying that the Bible only *contains* God's Word, the reader is given authority over the Bible, to pick and to choose those portions he or she believes truly *are* God's Word and to reject whatever other portions the reader does not personally like. In this way, you can feel free to believe anything you want. You can simply dismiss anything the Bible says in opposition to your personal belief as not being truly God's Word.)

This teaching becomes very attractive when the Church tries to mold itself after the world. For example, if you believe the Bible only *contains* God's Word, you can read it as if the miracles in the Bible were only myths. Thus, the miraculous six-day creation becomes a mere story rather than a miracle. This allows the creation story to be read in a way that accommodates, rather than rejects, the devil's lies concerning evolution.

Discuss: *How might the belief that the Bible only contains God's Word tempt you to doubt the certainty of your forgiveness of sins and salvation?* (Essentially, the conversation can boil down to this thought: if you are free to throw away this or that from the Bible, what will prevent you from throwing all of it away? If you cannot believe, for example, that Jonah was actually swallowed by a fish, what will prevent you from not believing that Christ rose from the dead? By saying that the Bible only contains God's Word, the reader has no certainty about what part of the Bible truly is God's Word.)

In the Word

Consider how the following ELCA practices and topics of theological conversation measure up to what the Bible teaches. Each of these conversations is made possible by the assumption that the Bible only contains God's Word, but is not itself God's Word.

The ordination of women

1 Timothy 2:11–14—Here Paul states that women must not exercise spiritual authority over men, as would be the case if a woman were a pastor. The reasons for this, according to Paul, have to do both with the order of creation and with the fall into sin. Many people do not like this prohibition. The idea that the Bible only contains God's Word allows you to throw out 1 Timothy 2:11–14 as being not from God but from a male chauvinist apostle.

Homosexuality as an acceptable alternative lifestyle for Christians

Romans 1:24–26—Here Paul states that homosexuality is not the result of a life lived by faith but exists "because they exchanged the truth about God for a lie."

1 Corinthians 6:9–10—"Men who practice homosexuality" without repenting and turning away from their sins to faith in Christ will not inherit eternal life.

The notion that the Bible only contains God's Word allows these passages and others like them to be discarded by those who wish to teach that homosexuality is an acceptable lifestyle for Christians.

Abortion

Jeremiah 1:5—God knows us before we are formed in the womb; He consecrates before we are even born.

Psalm 139:16—God sees and knows the "unformed substance" of a child in the womb.

Micah 6:7—Many times, people get abortions because of bad decisions or mistakes they make when they fall into sexual temptation. Micah asks if the fruit of the body (which, in the case of abortion, would be the unborn child) should be offered as a sacrifice for the sins of the soul. The answer, of course, is no. Jesus gave His life for the sins of the soul.

Discuss: *Is it always easy to understand why God would prohibit these things?* (Class participants may find it easy to see why God would prohibit abortion. It might not be so clear why God would prohibit homosexuality, especially in today's culture. Even more difficult would be the prohibition against women's ordination. While the Bible contains many things that are difficult to understand, we must simply accept them by faith. For example, no brain can comprehend how two natures [the divine and human] could unite in Christ—but they did! We also might not understand why Christ had to die so horribly to pay the price of forgiveness. Yet still we believe these things that do not make rational, logical sense to us.)

Discuss: *Why might it be important for Christians to believe and trust what God says in His Word, the Bible, even when we cannot fully understand why He might have said it?* (Answers may vary. The point boils down to this: "These are written so that you may believe" [John 20:31].)

Closing Prayer

Almighty God, give us grace that we may cast away the works of darkness and put upon ourselves the armor of light now in the time of this mortal life in which Your Son, Jesus Christ, came to visit us in great humility, that in the Last Day, when He shall come again in glorious majesty to judge both the living and the dead, we may rise to life immortal. Amen. *(LSB, p. 311)*

14 Evangelical Lutheran Church in American

A Message from Martin Luther

[God's Word] is called iron because of its inflexible and invincible straightness, or, as blessed Augustine has observed, its inflexible righteousness. For however many have tried to twist and bend the Word of God to their own interpretation, it has remained invincibly straight, convicting as liars those who have distorted it. . . . However, when some ascribe to the Scriptures the flexibility of a waxen nose and say that it is like a bending reed, this is due to the work of those who misuse the holy Word of God for their incompetent and unstable opinions. . . . They reach the point where the Word of God, which is fitting for everything, fits nothing. (LW 14:338)

Opening Prayer

L: No prophecy of Scripture comes from someone's own interpretation.

P: **For no prophecy was ever produced by the will of man,**

L: But men spoke from God.

P: **They spoke from God as they were carried along by the Holy Spirit.** (2 Peter 1:20–21)

L: Open our eyes, O Lord, that we may behold wondrous things out of Your Word.

P: **Amen!**

The Lutheran Difference

What phrase does the Nicene Creed use to describe the Bible? Why do you suppose a statement about the Bible was included in this creed?

_____

What do the following passages from the Bible have to say about the Bible?

2 Timothy 3:16
_____

2 Peter 1:20–21
_____

2 Peter 3:15–16
_____

Revelation 22:18–19
_____

Why might it seem attractive to say that the Bible only *contains* God's Word, rather than that the Bible *is* God's Word?

_____

How might the belief that the Bible only *contains* God's Word tempt you to doubt the certainty of your forgiveness of sins and salvation?

_____

In the Word

Consider how the following ELCA practices and topics of theological conversation measure up to what the Bible teaches. Each of these conversations is made possible by the assumption that the Bible only contains God's Word, but is not itself God's Word.

The ordination of women
1 Timothy 2:11–14
_____

Homosexuality as an acceptable alternative lifestyle for Christians
Romans 1:24–26
_____

1 Corinthians 6:9–10
_____

Abortion
Jeremiah 1:5
_____

Psalm 139:16
_____

Micah 6:7
_____

Is it always easy to understand why God would prohibit these things?

_____

Why might it be important for Christians to believe and trust what God says in His Word, the Bible, even when we cannot fully understand why He might have said it?

_____

15

Pentecostalism/ Assemblies of God

Lesson Focus

In Christ, we have a sure salvation; eternal life with Him is certain. In this session, we focus primarily on the Pentecostal/ Assemblies of God teaching that Christ or the Holy Spirit will speak to you apart from His written Word. But when you hear "voices" in your head or heart, you have no certainty that those voices are from God. Only those may feel certain who listen to God's voice through His written Word, the Bible.

Historical Context

Pentecostalism is a twentieth-century movement, tracing its modern history to a revival meeting that took place in Los Angeles, California, on April 14, 1906 (called the Azusa Street Revival). During this meeting, worshipers began to speak in strange languages, and this was attributed to the prompting of the Holy Spirit. As the movement spread and congregations formed, some of these congregations created larger organizations, such as today's United Pentecostal Church and the General Council of the Assemblies of God. Other Pentecostal congregations prefer to remain completely independent. Many Pentecostals are both Arminian and millennialist. They believe in the direct speaking of the Holy Spirit to the human heart (apart from the written Word) and, of course, in such manifestations as tongues and prophecy.

The Assemblies of God, which is the largest Pentecostal group today, was created in Hot Springs, Arkansas, in 1914. Where some Pentecostal groups are somewhat reclusive and separatist, the Assemblies of God has a strong missionary emphasis.

While most Pentecostal groups believe that God is Father, Son, and Holy Spirit, there is a strand of Pentecostalism commonly called "the Oneness Pentecostals" who deny the Trinity. While these Pentecostals are happy to use the name *Christian* to describe themselves, they are really a different religion rather than a Christian church body.

Distribute copies of Participant Page 15 and begin together. You may also want to hand out copies of the Quick Comparison Chart at this time.

A Message from Martin Luther

We must firmly hold that God grants His Spirit or grace to no one except through or with the preceding outward Word [Galatians 3:2, 5]. This protects us from the enthusiasts (i.e., souls who boast that they have the Spirit without and before the Word). They judge Scripture or the spoken Word and explain and stretch it at their pleasure. . . . Many still do this today. (SA III VIII 3)

Opening Prayer

L: They have Moses and the Prophets; let them hear them. (Luke 16:29)

P: If they do not hear Moses and the Prophets, neither will they be convinced if someone should rise from the dead. (Luke 16:31)

L: If anyone adds to [the prophecy of this book],

P: God will add to him the plagues described in this book. (Revelation 22:18)

L: Open our eyes, O Lord, that we may behold wondrous things out of Your Word.

P: Amen!

Miracles!

Continue working together through the questions and readings on the Participant Page. While there are varieties of "miraculous" gifts that the Pentecostals claim are still operating in the Church today, the most basic gift is what might be called "a personal prayer language." Pentecostals believe that when a Christian is filled with the Holy Spirit, the Spirit will miraculously give that person the power to speak in an unknown, unlearned tongue. If you cannot speak in tongues, your inability to do so means you do not have the Spirit's power!

What do the following Bible passages give as evidence that a Christian truly has God's Spirit within, apart from speaking in tongues?

Romans 8:9—All who belong to God have the Spirit of God within them. The Spirit dwells in all believers.

1 Corinthians 12:3—The simple fact that you believe and confess "Jesus is Lord" is God's sign and proof that you have the Holy Spirit in you.

Galatians 5:22–23—When good fruits are produced in your heart and mind, these are the fruits of the Spirit. For example, when you find yourself able to forgive others for their sins against you, this is a sign that God the Holy Spirit has created faith in you so that you also believe that you yourself are forgiven.

Discuss: *What sorts of fears or uncertainties might arise in you if you seek to speak in strange tongues, but fail to receive the "gift"?* (If you do not start speaking in this strange language, you might even pretend to have the gift of tongues. Worst of all, this failure to receive a "prayer language" can make you fear that God the Holy Spirit refuses to come to you. This creates doubt, uncertainty, and terror—not faith!)

What do the following passages say about how God gives you His Holy Spirit?

John 3:5 (Compare Ephesians 4:4–5.)—In Baptism you receive "water and the Spirit." This stands against the Pentecostal teaching that there are two Baptisms, one of water and one of the Spirit. But what does it say in Ephesians? "There is . . . one Baptism."

1 Corinthians 12:13 (Compare Titus 3:5–8.)—Again, Baptism is the key to receiving the Holy Spirit because "in one Spirit we were all baptized into one body."

Matthew 3:13–17—Pastors will often use the Baptism of our Lord as an analogy for every Christian's Baptism. This is a good analogy. Not only did God the Father adopt you to be His beloved child in your Baptism, but God the Holy Spirit also descended upon you to remain with you forever.

According to Acts 2:4–12, what special role did miraculous tongues play in the lives of the earliest Christians? (Tongues were not used as "a personal prayer language," but as a way of spreading the Gospel of our Lord very quickly throughout the world. Other miraculous gifts were given for the purpose of demonstrating that the teachings of the apostles were truly from God. These miracles were necessary because the New Testament was not yet in hand. That is to say, the apostles could not yet open the Gospel of Matthew, for example, point to a verse, and say, "This is what the Lord says.")

Discuss: *Why might this special role not be so helpful to the Church today?* (Now that the Scriptures have been fully written and given to the Church, we have one source to which we can point and say, "This is what God says." We no longer need miraculous signs such as those the apostles performed to demonstrate the truth of their preaching. The truth of Christian preaching today is demonstrated by God's Word, the Bible.)

In the Word

A second aspect of Pentecostal teaching, related to the first, is the assumption that the Holy Spirit will speak directly to your heart and mind apart from God's written Word, the Bible.

Discuss: *If you should hear a voice inside your head or heart that you think might be the voice of the Holy Spirit, how can you know for certain that it truly is the Spirit?* (The main point is that there is no way to be certain if the voice you hear in your head comes from the Holy Spirit, a demon sent by the devil, or from indigestion of last evening's meal. Many people have been horribly deceived by what they thought was the Holy Spirit speaking—but how could they know, apart from God's Word, the Bible?)

What warning does 2 Corinthians 11:14–15 provide about Satan's deceptions? (Because the devil masquerades as an angel of light, even those things that seem nice and good can be his evil deceptions. This is why, in matters of faith and worship, Christians entrust themselves only to the words and promises of God written in His Word, the Bible.)

What help does Hebrews 1:1–2 provide? ("In these last days He [God] has spoken to us by His Son." The Greek verb used for "has spoken" is called an "aorist" verb. It indicates fully completed action. This Bible verse announces that God has spoken once and for all through His Son, Jesus, whose words are recorded

in the New Testament. This is the final and complete speaking from God, and the Holy Spirit will not be saying anything other than what is written here. For further exploration, read John 14:26. According to that verse, the Holy Spirit's speaking consists of reminding us about what Jesus has already said. It does not consist of speaking apart from God's Word, the Bible.)

Discuss: *Why do you suppose the Holy Spirit is confessed in the Apostles' and Nicene creeds as an article of faith? What does Hebrews 11:1 have to say about faith?* (Many people want to feel the Holy Spirit in their heart or hear Him in their mind. But the Holy Spirit is an article of faith, that is, someone in whom we believe without seeing or feeling His presence. If we could feel His presence, we would no longer need to believe.)

Discuss: *If you want to be sure and certain beyond all doubt that you are hearing the Holy Spirit speak to you, where might you direct your attention?* (In the end, the conversation needs to conclude that we can only be certain that the Holy Spirit is speaking when we listen to the Word.)

Closing Prayer

Almighty God, send Your Holy Spirit into our hearts that He may rule and direct us according to Your will, comfort us in all our temptations and afflictions, defend us from all error, and lead us into all truth that we, being steadfast in faith, may increase in all good works and in the end obtain everlasting life; through Jesus Christ, our Lord. Amen. (*LSB*, p. 310)

15 Pentecostalism/ Assemblies of God

A Message from Martin Luther

We must firmly hold that God grants His Spirit or grace to no one except through or with the preceding outward Word [Galatians 3:2, 5]. This protects us from the enthusiasts (i.e., souls who boast that they have the Spirit without and before the Word). They judge Scripture or the spoken Word and explain and stretch it at their pleasure. . . . Many still do this today. (SA III VIII 3)

Opening Prayer

L: They have Moses and the Prophets; let them hear them. (Luke 16:29)

P: If they do not hear Moses and the Prophets, neither will they be convinced if someone should rise from the dead. (Luke 16:31)

L: If anyone adds to [the prophecy of this book],

P: God will add to him the plagues described in this book. (Revelation 22:18)

L: Open our eyes, O Lord, that we may behold wondrous things out of Your Word.

P: Amen!

Miracles!

What do the following Bible passages give as evidence that a Christian truly has God's Spirit within, apart from speaking in tongues?

Romans 8:9

1 Corinthians 12:3

Galatians 5:22–23

What sorts of fears or uncertainties might arise in you if you seek to speak in strange tongues, but fail to receive the "gift"?

What do the following passages say about how God gives you His Holy Spirit?

John 3:5 (Compare Ephesians 4:4–5.)

1 Corinthians 12:13 (Compare Titus 3:5–8.)

Matthew 3:13–17

According to **Acts 2:4–12,** what special role did miraculous tongues play in the lives of the earliest Christians?

Why might this special role not be so helpful to the Church today?

In the Word

If you should hear a voice inside your head or heart that you think might be the voice of the Holy Spirit, how can you know for certain that it truly is the Spirit?

What warning does **2 Corinthians 11:14–15** provide about Satan's deceptions?

What help does **Hebrews 1:1–2** provide?

Why do you suppose the Holy Spirit is confessed in the Apostles' and Nicene creeds as an article of faith? What does **Hebrews 11:1** have to say about faith?

If you want to be sure and certain beyond all doubt that you are hearing the Holy Spirit speak to you, where might you direct your attention?

Participant Page 15 *One Christ, Many Creeds* copyright © 2008 Concordia Publishing House. Scripture: ESV® *Concordia: The Lutheran Confessions,* second edition, copyright © 2006 Concordia Publishing House. All rights reserved. Reproduced by permission.

16

Emerging Churches

© Shutterstock/Brian Dunne

Lesson Focus

In Christ, we have a sure salvation; eternal life with Him is certain. In this session, we focus primarily on the root cause of the "Emergent Churches," which essentially is the search for something new. This search for newness, however, causes you to look for a sense of spiritual or religious fulfillment in some place other than the clear Word of God. This search, apart from clear truth claims of the Bible, carries grave dangers. Among the greatest dangers is that you end up taking your eyes off Jesus, the one true source of certainty and assurance.

Historical Context

The Emergent (or Emerging) Church is probably better thought of as a movement rather than a specific church body in the formal sense of the term. There is not much history to trace for this movement, either, as it is a product of the twenty-first century. Because of this newness, and because of its philosophical assumptions, it is hard to state definitively the teachings of the Emergent Church groups.

The major hope of the Emergent Church groups is to reach, to engage in conversation, and to incorporate into a worship experience those people who do not feel able to connect with a traditional church body. Many of those who feel unable to connect with a traditional church body find it difficult to accept the exclusive truth claims of the Bible. Generally speaking, these individuals are influenced by a philosophy called "postmodernism," which holds that truth is individualized and primarily based on your own opinion or worldview. (Essentially, postmodernism claims that your "truth" may be the opposite of my "truth," but both "truths" are equally valid.)

The acronym *EPIC* is often used to describe the main points of emphasis in the Emergent Church:

Experiential—Christianity must provide a religious feeling or experience in order to get people involved.

Participatory—Worship should not be something you receive, but something you give.

Image-based—The message of the Christian faith is more appealing when it is conveyed through streaming video, drama, artwork, and so on.

Communal—There is a strong feeling of togetherness, or of being part of a larger community.

Distribute copies of Participant Page 16. Begin by reading the quote from Luther and then the responsive Opening Prayer.

A Message from Martin Luther

The world cannot stand on the things that are present, and it is always tormented by the things that are in the future. So it is that Germany is always looking for something new. When the Gospel began, everyone ran to it eagerly; but once the Gospel has prevailed, we are bored and forget the great blessings. Now there is a rush for the Sacramentarians [that is, a group of false teachers who denied Christ's presence in the Lord's Supper]; but when they have grown old, people will become bored with them and will want something else. (LW 15:144)

Opening Prayer

L: All things are full of weariness; a man cannot utter it;

P: The eye is not satisfied with seeing, nor the ear filled with hearing.

L: What has been is what will be, and what has been done is what will be done,

P: And there is nothing new under the sun.
   (Ecclesiastes 1:8–9)

L: Open our eyes, O Lord, that we may behold wondrous things out of Your Word.

P: Amen!

Emerging Experience

The Emergent Church focuses on the importance of religious experiences and active, individual participation in worship. Through these participatory experiences, the Emergent Church hopes to provide a new form of Christianity.

Discuss: *What elements in Ecclesiastes 1:1–11 reflect the complaint of those who are attracted to the Emergent Church? According to this same passage, in what way is it impossible truly to find something new?* (In Ecclesiastes, Solomon found himself so bored with the world that he complained that everything was useless. Many people who are attracted to the Emergent Church feel similarly dissatisfied and are searching for something that will make them feel different. Yet this search for a sense of fulfillment or satisfaction is like chasing after the wind. Once you finally arrive at the way you want to feel, the feeling eludes you again, and you must resume your search.)

According to John 6:22–26, why did large crowds follow Jesus wherever He went? What happened in John 6:35–60 that caused many people to stop following Jesus? (The crowds were attracted to Jesus not because of His teachings, but because He was able to fill their bellies. Stated another way, the crowds followed Jesus because He was giving them what they felt they wanted. However, when Jesus began to teach them the Word of God, many began to turn away. They did not want God's powerful and living Word; they just wanted full bellies.)

What do the following verses have to say about those who seek religious experiences?

Matthew 12:38–41—Jesus warns that those who want experiential religion should be careful. "An evil and adulterous generation seeks for a sign" (v. 39). All of the signs necessary for faith and salvation are provided in this: as Jonah was swallowed by the fish, "so will the Son of Man be three days and three nights in the heart of the earth" (v. 40).

Matthew 24:3–14—The disciples also wanted to experience a sign to know that Jesus was truly God.

1 Corinthians 1:22–25—Those who want to experience special signs end up stumbling on the crucifixion.

John 20:26–29—Jesus rebuked Thomas's desire for a religious experience, declaring, "Blessed are those who have not seen and yet have believed."

Discuss: *In what way can the pursuit of religious experiences lead Christians into great danger? Use 2 Timothy 4:3–5 to guide your discussion.* (The search for a religious experience can be like a drug addiction: you can never get enough. Once the thrill of one experience has passed, you must search for another. This might be part of the reason why worship forms in the Emergent Church are highly eclectic and unusual. The worshipers have come there to find their next experience. However, Paul warns in 2 Timothy that those who search for something new—something they like—end up falling away from the faith.)

Whose Truth?

The Emergent Church is built on the post-modern assumption that truth is relative to the individual. Stated another way, you can personally believe whatever you want to believe (call it "your truth") and I can personally believe what I want to believe (call it "my truth") and both "truths" are equally valid.

According to the following Bible passages, what is the source of all truth?

Psalm 119:151–52—God's truth comes from God's Word, not from what individuals might personally dream up as truth.

John 17:17—Jesus prayed to the heavenly Father, "Your Word is truth."

Romans 1:25—When Christians do not stick close to the clear truth of God's Word, the Bible, they end up exchanging the truth about God for a lie.

Romans 3:4—It is better that God be called true and every person a liar than to substitute a person's own ideas about what is true for God's truth.

According to John 8:44, what is the source of every idea that opposes God's truth? (Every idea that opposes God's truth, even a good-sounding idea, is a lie from the father of lies, the devil.)

Discuss: *In what way might the postmodern idea of individual truth be usable, or even important, for everyday life? In what way is it disastrous to the life of the Christian faith?* (In everyday life, postmodernism might prove to be a helpful way of opening conversations concerning Christ with your friends. That is to say, in America, everyone has the right to believe what they want to believe. After hearing their thoughts and ideas about religion, you then could speak about what you believe is true. Granting the postmodern assumption that all people's ideas are worthy of contemplation and thought, you could then counter with the same claim that your thoughts are also valuable for conversation and contemplation.

When you build a church body on the postmodern concept of truth, however, you are actually building that church body on uncertainty. How can you ever be certain of your forgiveness and salvation if you must dream up for yourself what it means to be saved, what is sin, and so on?)

In what way do the following Bible verses describe true Christian communion, or fellowship, one with another?

Ephesians 2:20—Our communal connection with our fellow Christians starts with the fact that we are "built on the foundation of the apostles and prophets," that is, the words of the Old and New Testaments in the Bible.

1 Corinthians 10:14–22—Christ joins us together in communal fellowship in the Lord's Supper. Could the Emergent Church's desire for a communal life be rooted in the disbelief that the Lord's Supper miraculously creates our communion?

Closing Prayer

Blessed Lord, You have caused all Holy Scriptures to be written for our learning. Grant that we may so hear them, read, mark, learn, and inwardly digest them that, by patience and comfort of Your holy Word, we may embrace and ever hold fast the blessed hope of everlasting life; through Jesus Christ, our Lord. Amen. (*LSB*, p. 308)

16 Emerging Churches

A Message from Martin Luther

The world cannot stand on the things that are present, and it is always tormented by the things that are in the future. So it is that Germany is always looking for something new. When the Gospel began, everyone ran to it eagerly; but once the Gospel has prevailed, we are bored and forget the great blessings. Now there is a rush for the Sacramentarians [that is, a group of false teachers who denied Christ's presence in the Lord's Supper]; but when they have grown old, people will become bored with them and will want something else. (LW 15:144)

Opening Prayer

L: All things are full of weariness; a man cannot utter it;

P: The eye is not satisfied with seeing, nor the ear filled with hearing.

L: What has been is what will be, and what has been done is what will be done,

P: And there is nothing new under the sun.

(Ecclesiastes 1:8–9)

L: Open our eyes, O Lord, that we may behold wondrous things out of Your Word.

P: Amen!

Emerging Experience

What elements in **Ecclesiastes 1:1–11** reflect the complaint of those who are attracted to the Emergent Church? According to this same passage, in what way is it impossible truly to find something new?

_____

According to **John 6:22–26**, why did large crowds follow Jesus wherever He went? What happened in **John 6:35–60** that caused many people to stop following Jesus?

What do the following verses have to say about those who seek religious experiences?

Matthew 12:38–41
_____

Matthew 24:3–14
_____

1 Corinthians 1:22–25
_____

John 20:26–29
_____

In what way can the pursuit of religious experiences lead Christians into great danger? Use **2 Timothy 4:3–5** to guide your discussion.

_____

Whose Truth?

According to the following Bible passages, what is the source of all truth?

Psalm 119:151–52
_____

John 17:17
_____

Romans 1:25
_____

Romans 3:4
_____

According to **John 8:44**, what is the source of every idea that opposes God's truth?

_____

In what way might the postmodern idea of individual truth be usable, or even important, for everyday life? In what way is it disastrous to the life of the Christian faith?

_____

In what way do the following Bible verses describe true Christian communion, or fellowship, one with another?

Ephesians 2:20
_____

1 Corinthians 10:14–22
_____

Participant Page 16 *One Christ, Many Creeds* copyright © 2008 Concordia Publishing House. Scripture: ESV® Luther's Works, American Edition: vol. 15 copyright © 1972 Concordia Publishing House. All rights reserved. Reproduced by permission.

Church Body

The Lutheran Church—Missouri Synod

History

The Lutheran Church—Missouri Synod was formed in 1847 by twelve pastors and fifteen congregations as "The German Evangelical Lutheran Synod of Missouri, Ohio, and Other States."

Vital Statistics

The LCMS has approximately 2.5 million members. The international headquarters is located in St. Louis, Missouri. Source: www.lcms.org.

Source of Doctrine

The LCMS bases its doctrine on the inerrant Word of God found in the Scriptures and, as an exposition of the Scriptures, the Lutheran Confessions found in the Book of Concord.

Role of Christ/Way of Salvation

Salvation is a free gift given by grace through faith in Christ Jesus. Even faith is a free gift of God that humankind plays no role in. We simply receive the free gift of faith through the Word and in our Baptism. Salvation is found in Christ alone.

Sacraments

Baptism bestows forgiveness, rescue from death and the devil, and the gift of faith to eternal salvation. In Holy Communion, the communicant receives the true body and blood of Christ in, with, and under the bread and the wine for forgiveness and strengthening of faith.

One Christ, Many Creeds © 2008 Concordia Publishing House. Permission granted to purchaser to reproduce this page for use in educational settings. All other rights reserved.

The Roman Catholic Church

History

The Roman Catholic Church traces its founding to Matthew 16:13–20, where Jesus tells Peter, "I tell you, you are Peter, and on this rock I will build My church. . . . I will give you the keys of the kingdom of heaven." Church tradition teaches that Peter became the first bishop of the Church in Rome. In 330, the Roman emperor Constantine moved the center of the empire to Byzantium, naming it Constantinople in honor of himself. Constantine and succeeding emperors used the power of the Church to further their own rule, thus blurring the line between church and state even further. The congregation in Rome became the most powerful in the western part of the empire. The bishop of the Church in Rome was called "pope" after the Latin word for "father." Today's popes claim an unbroken line of succession back to Peter.

Vital Statistics

The Roman Catholic Church is the largest church body in America with more than 69 million members. The Roman Catholic Church is highly structured, with the sole "headquarters" based within the city-state of Vatican City in Rome. Sources: www.vatican.va; www.usccb.org.

Source of Doctrine

Rome bases its doctrine on the Scriptures (including the deuterocanonical books) and oral tradition as preserved in ancient writings. The church has the authority to establish doctrine through either churchwide ecumenical councils or the teachings/writings of the pope himself.

Role of Christ/Way of Salvation

Roman Catholics teach that at Baptism God gives sinners a saving righteousness they can use to help themselves in the face of God's judgment. Saving righteousness is made evident and increased by doing good works to merit more and more grace and eternal life.

Rome also teaches that while forgiveness of sin is granted because of Christ's suffering and death, sinners still make amends to the majesty of God offended by sin through acts of penance.

Sacraments

The Roman Catholic Church observes seven sacraments. Like Lutherans, Catholics celebrate Baptism and Holy Communion (Eucharist). Baptism is generally performed on infants, granting forgiveness to the recipient. The Eucharist (Holy Communion) also contains the real presence, but Rome teaches that the bread and wine are transformed in their very substance into body and blood. In addition, Roman Catholics celebrate confirmation as the sacrament in which the Holy Spirit is bestowed on the believer. Penance gives remission of guilt and punishment through specific acts of contrition, confession, and satisfaction for sin. These can involve prayer, the Mass, fasting, merciful acts, and others as assigned by the priest. Matrimony honors the divine institution of marriage, declaring marriages performed outside of the church invalid. Holy orders is the sacrament celebrated only by individuals at their ordination into the service of the church. Anointing of the sick involves prayers and anointing with holy oils for the seriously ill.

Lutheran Response

Roman Catholics confess Jesus Christ as the way to salvation. When you talk to members of the Catholic Church, begin with statements that encompass the common elements of our faith. Avoid temptations to compromise biblical teaching just for the sake of fellowship. Not all Roman Catholics will necessarily believe all the official teachings of the church concerning individual doctrines. Use Scripture as your source when addressing areas of difference between Lutherans and Catholics.

One Christ, Many Creeds © 2008 Concordia Publishing House. Permission granted to purchaser to reproduce this page for use in educational settings. All other rights reserved.

Church Body

Eastern Orthodox Churches

(Greek Orthodox Archdiocese of America, the Orthodox Church in America)

History

The Eastern Orthodox Church arose following the split between East and West in 1054 due to doctrinal and political strife. Geographic and language isolation developed the Orthodox Church along nationalistic lines. The Greek (Greek Orthodox Archdiocese of America) and Russian (Orthodox Church in America) divisions are the primary groups in the United States.

Vital Statistics

The Greek Orthodox Archdiocese of America has 1.5 million members, while the Orthodox Church in America has 1 million; overall there are 250 million Orthodox believers worldwide. The Greek Orthodox Archdiocese is headquartered in New York City, with eight metropolises in New Jersey, Chicago, Atlanta, Detroit, San Francisco, Pittsburgh, Boston, and Denver. The Orthodox Church in America has its headquarters in Syosset, New York. Note that the Orthodox Church does not celebrate Easter at the same time as the Western Church. Sources: www.oca.org; www.goarch.org.

Source of Doctrine

The Orthodox Church accepts the Scriptures, including select apocryphal books (Tobit, Judith, Sirach, and others). They also include oral traditions of Christ and His apostles. Eastern Orthodox churches teach that tradition completes and explains Scripture. The teachings of the church as a whole are placed on the same level as Scripture.

Role of Christ/Way of Salvation

Orthodoxy teaches that man is fallen and corrupt, but not dead in sin. It believes that our will cooperates with God in bringing about conversion and faith. It also teaches that, while Christ died for our salvation, the believer contributes to his or her justification through good works.

Sacraments

Like the Roman Catholic Church, the Orthodox Church teaches seven sacraments, though with a few distinct differences. While Baptism is performed on infants, it involves a threefold immersion. Chrismation (Confirmation) involves anointing with oil and is accompanied by the Eucharist. Holy Communion uses leavened bread since they believe that is what Jesus used. The Orthodox Church practices intinction, where the bread is dipped into wine and given to the worshiper on a spoon.

Lutheran Response

Like the Catholic Church, the Eastern Orthodox Church shares many of our beliefs. However, we have serious differences in our understanding of the sacraments and the worship of the saints. Approach Orthodox believers with a thorough understanding of the Scriptures and what we teach.

One Christ, Many Creeds © 2008 Concordia Publishing House. Permission granted to purchaser to reproduce this page for use in educational settings. All other rights reserved.

Church Body

Presbyterian Churches

History

The Presbyterian churches were founded in the Reformation era based on the writings of John Calvin and John Knox. Presbyterian ministers were among the early settlers of America as well as signers of the Declaration of Independence. Through the years, the various Presbyterian churches have split and re-formed. The Presbyterian Church USA is the largest group in North America.

Vital Statistics

Churches are governed by presbyters (elders). Lay elders and teaching elders (pastors) conduct the affairs of the church. There are approximately 2.4 million members of the Presbyterian Church. National offices are located in Louisville, Kentucky. Source: www.pcusa.org.

Source of Doctrine

Scripture serves as the source for doctrine. Presbyterians observe the Westminster Confession as a statement of their beliefs. The writings of Calvin and Knox influence the teachings of the Presbyterian Church.

Role of Christ/Way of Salvation

Justification comes by grace through faith. Salvation is seen as God's generous gift to the believer, not the result of anything the individual has done. However, in the Calvinist viewpoint, this gift comes on its own, without a means of grace (i.e., Word and Sacraments). This leaves the believer to decide if the promise of God's grace is really for him or her. Presbyterians teach "once saved, always saved."

Sacraments

Since Baptism and Holy Communion are not seen as means of grace, these Sacraments take on a merely symbolic role in the Presbyterian Church.

Lutheran Response

While the Presbyterian Church also emerged from the Reformation, its understanding of faith and salvation does differ from Lutheranism. Careful discussion and clear explanation are required.

One Christ, Many Creeds © 2008 Concordia Publishing House. Permission granted to purchaser to reproduce this page for use in educational settings. All other rights reserved.

Church Body

Christian Reformed Churches/Evangelical Free Church

History

The Christian Reformed Church traces its roots to the reformer John Calvin. The CRC split from the Dutch Reformed Church before the leaders moved to America. The postwar era brought about growth and change in the CRC as the church focused on looking outward.

The Evangelical Free Church in America formed in 1950 from the merger of the Swedish Evangelical Free Church and the Norwegian-Danish Free Church Association. The EFCA consists of 1,300 independent congregations in an organized association.

Vital Statistics

These two church bodies together have approximately 620,000 members (EFCA: 340,000; CRCNA: 278,000). The Christian Reformed Church is headquartered in Grand Rapids, Michigan. The Evangelical Free Church national office is located in Minneapolis, Minnesota. Sources: www.crcna.org; www.efca.org.

Source of Doctrine

The Christian Reformed Church accepts the inspired Word of God as the supreme and final authority on all matters on which it speaks. It also subscribes to the three universal creeds of the Church. In addition, the church recognizes the Belgic Confession, the Canons of Dort, and the Heidelberg Catechism as expositions of their confessions.

The Evangelical Free Church also views the Scriptures as the source of final authority for Christian faith and life. The church has officially adopted a twelve-article Statement of Faith that outlines the church's basic teachings.

Role of Christ/Way of Salvation

Like most Reformed churches, the CRC and EFCA describe the way of salvation in terms of the result of faith received as a gift from God and earned by the suffering, death, and resurrection of Jesus Christ. The decision to accept faith is made by the believer.

Sacraments

Baptism and the Lord's Supper are both celebrated as ordinances that believers must observe, but they do not serve as means of salvation.

Lutheran Response

While the Lutheran and Reformed Churches share their respect for the Scriptures, Reformed believers do not share in our understanding of the benefits of the Sacraments. Any discussion must come from a mutual respect for God's Word.

One Christ, Many Creeds © 2008 Concordia Publishing House. Permission granted to purchaser to reproduce this page for use in educational settings. All other rights reserved.

Church Body

The Anglican Episcopal Church

History

This church was founded by King Henry VIII in 1534 when he declared the English church to be independent of the pope. All of the church bodies that resulted from this split are called the Anglican Communion. Called the Church of England in Europe, it is called the Episcopal Church in the United States.

Vital Statistics

The Episcopal Church has about 2.33 million members in the United States. They are headquartered in New York City. The Episcopal Church allows for the ordination of women and, in recent years, openly homosexual individuals. Source: www.episcopalchurch.org.

Source of Doctrine

The Anglican Communion is directed by Thirty-Nine Articles of Faith formulated in 1563 under Queen Elizabeth I to include differing viewpoints while avoiding extremes. As a result, the Articles are interpreted differently by each of the Anglican bodies. Every ten years, the Anglican Communion meets in the Lambeth Conference to review these statements.

Role of Christ/Way of Salvation

While the Episcopal Church teaches that we are justified through the work of Christ, it leaves room for participation on the part of the believer.

Sacraments

The Episcopal Church practices a trinitarian Baptism for all ages. It teaches that through Baptism the baptized becomes part of the community of faith. The Eucharist shares the real presence of Christ's body and blood as a symbol of the unity of all believers.

Lutheran Response

Episcopal believers may vary widely in their personal statements of faith. Our opposition to the ordination of homosexuals and women stands against any common ground. Approach the Episcopal believer with a thorough understanding of the Scripture on these issues.

One Christ, Many Creeds © 2008 Concordia Publishing House. Permission granted to purchaser to reproduce this page for use in educational settings. All other rights reserved.

Church Body

Methodist Churches

History

The Methodist Church traces its history to the work of brothers John and Charles Wesley. The Wesleys served as missionaries to the Georgia colonies from the Church of England in 1736. Having both returned to England by 1738, the brothers started a renewal movement within the Church of England. By 1760, Methodism took root in America under the leadership of Robert Strawbridge. The Wesleys sent follow-up mission leaders who helped the Church grow across the nation. Methodists earned their name from their focus on methods and rules for holy living.

Vital Statistics

The United Methodist Church has 8.3 million members; the AME has 3.5 million; the AMEZ has 1.2 million; and the Christian MEC has 718,000. The United Methodist Church national office is located in Nashville, Tennessee. Sources: www.umc.org; www.c-m-e.org.

Source of Doctrine

Methodist churches root their teachings in their Articles of Religion, the Rules of the Methodist Church, and a collection of Wesley's sermons. Scripture is understood through the filter of Church tradition and the test of human reason. Methodists demonstrate a great tolerance for differences, especially concerning interpretation of Scripture.

Role of Christ/Way of Salvation

Methodists teach that believers are able to cooperate in their conversion. While they acknowledge God's role in forgiving sin and Jesus' work of obedience, they teach that Christians are enabled by sanctification to do their own holy works, which qualify them for eternal life.

Sacraments

While Methodists participate in the Sacraments of Baptism and Holy Communion, they are seen as divinely appointed activities in which people receive help from God. They are not seen as a means of grace by which the believer receives forgiveness.

Lutheran Response

Since the Methodist believer may not share the same understanding of Scripture, approach them with a spirit of love and concern.. Be prepared to thoroughly explain what Lutherans teach as part of this conversation.

One Christ, Many Creeds © 2008 Concordia Publishing House. Permission granted to purchaser to reproduce this page for use in educational settings. All other rights reserved.

Church Body

The Salvation Army

History

The Salvation Army was started in the slums of London in the 1860s by William Booth and his wife, Catherine. They reached out to those considered the lowest of British society. The first Salvationists in the United States started their work in 1880. From their earliest days, the Salvationists have used military titles for leaders and followers in the church. The Salvation Army has combined spiritual care with social work since its inception.

Vital Statistics

Members call themselves Salvationists. There are 446,000 members in the United States. Source: www.salvationarmyusa.org.

Source of Doctrine

Salvationists accept only the divinely inspired Word of God in the Old and New Testaments as the source for all teaching and preaching. Before enlisting as Salvation Army "soldiers," prospective Salvationist members must sign the "Articles of War," a document outlining their basic beliefs.

Role of Christ/Way of Salvation

The Salvation Army teaches that salvation comes through the work of Jesus Christ on the cross. Salvation is a free gift of God's grace through faith. However, Salvationists also believe that man can make a conscious decision to come to faith. Therefore, members enlist as "soldiers" in the Salvation Army. Salvationists also teach that it is possible for man to overcome sin and obtain perfection on his own.

Sacraments

Salvationists do not observe any sacraments.

Lutheran Response

While we highly regard the charitable support provided by the Salvation Army, we differ in our understanding of how we come to faith. Approach the Salvationist firmly grounded in the Word of God.

One Christ, Many Creeds © 2008 Concordia Publishing House. Permission granted to purchaser to reproduce this page for use in educational settings. All other rights reserved.

Church Body

Church of the Nazarene

History

The Church of the Nazarene shares its roots with other Protestant churches in the Wesleyan and Holiness traditions. The first Church of the Nazarene was established in 1895 in Los Angeles. Through the years, the church has combined with and separated from other Pentecostal and Holiness denominations as it spread from the West Coast, across the United States, and into many foreign countries.

Vital Statistics

The Church of the Nazarene has 645,000 members. Its national and international offices are in Kansas City, Missouri. Source: www.nazarene.org.

Source of Doctrine

The Church of the Nazarene accepts the inerrant Scriptures as its main source of doctrine. The church's essential teachings are described in the Articles of Faith, the General Rules, and the Articles of Organization and Government, which have been adopted by the church's General Assembly.

Role of Christ/Way of Salvation

The Nazarene Church teaches that salvation is a free gift of God given to the believer. Once the individual confesses his or her sin and is made free from original sin, the heart of the believer must be fully cleansed through the Baptism of the Holy Spirit. Nazarenes teach that at the final judgment each person shall appear before God to be judged according to his or her deeds in this life.

Sacraments

The Church of the Nazarene observes Baptism as a sign of the individual's acceptance of faith. It indicates his or her desire to lead an obedient, holy, and righteous life. Children may be baptized at their parents' request, as long as the parents promise to instruct them in the faith.

The Lord's Supper is practiced as a symbol or remembrance of Christ's institution of this Sacrament and as a visible reminder of His sacrifice on the cross.

Lutheran Response

The Nazarene understanding of salvation is grounded in a keeping of the Law. Any discussion of faith must be grounded in an understanding of God's Word, which clearly shows that Christ alone earned salvation for us.

One Christ, Many Creeds © 2008 Concordia Publishing House. Permission granted to purchaser to reproduce this page for use in educational settings. All other rights reserved.

Church Body

Baptist Churches

History

The first Baptist churches originated in the seventeenth century among the English Separatist (Congregationalist) believers. Many different Baptist church bodies exist within North America today, including historically black church bodies. With more than 16 million members, the Southern Baptist Convention is the largest Protestant denomination in America.

Vital Statistics

The American Baptist Churches USA has a membership of about 1.5 million; the National Baptist Convention of America, about 2.5 million; the National Baptist Convention, USA, about 7 million; the Progressive National Baptist Convention, about 500,000; and the Southern Baptist Convention, about 16.3 million. The Southern Baptist Convention is based in Nashville, Tennessee. Sources: www.abc-usa.org; www.nbcamerica.net; www.nationalbaptist.com; www.pnbc.org; www.sbc.net.

Source of Doctrine

Scripture is viewed as the source for belief. Most Baptist churches establish their own statement of faith that serves as an expression of beliefs that members must agree to in order to join the church.

Role of Christ/Way of Salvation

Salvation involves the redemption of the whole man and is offered freely to all who accept Jesus Christ as Lord and Savior, who by His own blood obtained eternal redemption for the believer. In its broadest sense, salvation includes regeneration, sanctification, and glorification. Salvation is a gift from God granted to the "elect," those chosen by God for salvation, but man plays a conscious role in "accepting" faith.

Sacraments

Christian Baptism is the immersion of a believer in water. It is an act of obedience symbolizing the believer's faith in a crucified, buried, and risen Savior, the believer's death to sin, the burial of the life, and the resurrection to walk in newness of life in Christ Jesus. Baptism of infants is not considered necessary since Baptism indicates an understanding and acceptance of faith in the Baptist viewpoint. The only valid form of Baptism in the Baptist churches is total immersion.

The Lord's Supper is a symbolic act of obedience whereby members memorialize the death of the Redeemer and anticipate His second coming.

While Baptists see both Baptism and the Lord's Supper as symbols, they are necessary symbols.

Lutheran Response

The difference in belief surrounding the purpose and form of Baptism serves as a major obstacle when approaching Baptist believers. A mutual understanding of the Scriptures would be a neutral ground from which to engage the Baptist believer in conversation.

One Christ, Many Creeds © 2008 Concordia Publishing House. Permission granted to purchaser to reproduce this page for use in educational settings. All other rights reserved.

Church Body

Mennonite Church

History

The Mennonite Church traces its heritage back to the early days of the Reformation. Saying that Luther's reforms didn't go far enough, early church leaders, like Menno Simons, encouraged followers to be rebaptized since they considered infant Baptism invalid. Called the Anabaptists, this movement eventually spun out into the Baptist, Mennonite, and other Protestant churches.

Vital Statistics

The Mennonite Church has about 114,000 members. Most Mennonites opt out of military service since they subscribe to a strong belief in world peace. Mennonites also strongly defend the separation between church and state. The Mennonite Executive Leadership offices are located in Elkhart, Indiana, and Newton, Kansas. Source: www.mennoniteusa.org.

Source of Doctrine

Mennonites use Scripture to help define their faith. The Dordrecht Confession is the most widely used statement of faith in the Mennonite Church. At the same time, Mennonites look to the Holy Spirit for additional revelations in dreams to help them further define the faith.

Role of Christ/Way of Salvation

Mennonite believers teach that justification is made possible by the sacrifice of Jesus. At the same time, they teach that faith and the good works of the believer cooperate to provide salvation.

Sacraments

While they practice Baptism and Holy Communion, Mennonites do not view either as sacraments. Rather, each is considered a sign of a significant event in the believer's life. Baptism is a sign that the believer has repented of sins, received forgiveness, renounced evil, and died to sin. The Lord's Supper is seen as a sign of the renewed covenant between God and the believer. It also serves to join the body of believers together within the community of faith.

Lutheran Response

In talking with a Mennonite believer, it may be difficult to establish a common ground. The importance of sharing God's Word may provide a starting place for any conversation.

One Christ, Many Creeds © 2008 Concordia Publishing House. Permission granted to purchaser to reproduce this page for use in educational settings. All other rights reserved.

Seventh-day Adventist Church

History

The Seventh-day Adventist Church traces its beginnings to Washington, New Hampshire, in 1844. William Miller, a former Baptist preacher, and a series of individuals including some influential women began preaching a message of the impending "Second Advent" of Christ. They also stressed a need for the Christian Church to return to the historic seventh-day Sabbath. On May 21, 1863, the Seventh-day Adventist Church was officially organized with a total of 125 congregations. Today, they are a worldwide denomination with 90 percent of their membership outside of North America.

Vital Statistics

The Seventh-day Adventist Church has more than 1 million members in the United States (14 million worldwide). Their General Conference headquarters is located in Silver Spring, Maryland. Source: www.adventist.org.

Source of Doctrine

Seventh-day Adventists accept the Bible as their only creed. From Scripture they set forth twenty-seven fundamental belief statements that have been adopted by their General Conference. Adventists believe that they are led by the Holy Spirit to a better understanding of Scripture.

Role of Christ/Way of Salvation

Adventists believe that the Holy Spirit leads them to repent of their sins and be renewed by faith in Jesus as Lord and Christ, as substitute and example. Faith comes through the divine power of God's Word as a gift of God's grace. The Spirit gives believers the power to live a holy life. The role of Christ is often neglected.

Sacraments

Baptism is performed by immersion only and serves as a symbol of our union with Christ. By Baptism, Adventists confess their faith in the death and resurrection of Jesus and testify of their death to sin and desire to walk in newness of life.

Adventists teach that the Lord's Supper is a participation in the elements of body and blood as an expression of faith. In Communion, Christ is present to meet and strengthen His people. The service of foot washing precedes the Lord's Supper to indicate renewed cleansing and willingness to serve others.

Lutheran Response

The majority of Adventist believers are likely unaware of all of the official teachings of their church body. Since they share our great love of the Scriptures, this is a common ground from which to approach the Adventist believer.

One Christ, Many Creeds © 2008 Concordia Publishing House. Permission granted to purchaser to reproduce this page for use in educational settings. All other rights reserved.

Church Body

United Church of Christ

(Congregational)

History

While the United Church of Christ was founded in 1957, its history dates back much further. The Pilgrims that settled Plymouth Colony first brought Congregationalism to America. They united with the Puritans under the Cambridge Platform of 1648.

Vital Statistics

The United Church of Christ has 1.3 million members in the United States. Its Office of the General Ministry is located in Cleveland, Ohio. Source: www.ucc.org.

Source of Doctrine

The United Church of Christ builds its doctrine on the Word of God, the creeds of the ecumenical councils, and the confessions of the Reformation (including the Augsburg Confession and Luther's Small Catechism). There is no centralized authority or hierarchy that can impose any doctrine or form of worship on its members. The UCC acknowledges the historic creeds and confessions of the Church as testimonies but not tests of the faith.

Role of Christ/Way of Salvation

Since the UCC results from so many different Reformed Church backgrounds, it is difficult to identify a clear statement concerning justification. The role of the believer in salvation is most often placed above Christ's role.

Sacraments

The UCC celebrates both Baptism and Holy Communion. Baptism is available for all ages and is seen as the baptized's entrance into the fellowship of believers. Through Baptism, a person receives the gift of the Spirit and forgiveness of sins. The UCC understanding of Communion varies greatly from the Lutheran perspective. They teach that through participation in the Sacrament of Communion, believers celebrate and remember Christ's sacrifice as they experience the fellowship of all believers. The elements (bread and wine) are seen as symbolic only—there is no teaching of the real presence.

Lutheran Response

The lack of sacramental teachings in the UCC leaves the believer without an understanding of the blessings they receive in Baptism and Communion. Be prepared to show this believer these benefits using the Word of God.

One Christ, Many Creeds © 2008 Concordia Publishing House. Permission granted to purchaser to reproduce this page for use in educational settings. All other rights reserved.

Church Body

Evangelical Lutheran Church in America

(ELCA)

History

The Evangelical Lutheran Church in America (ELCA) was established in 1988 as a result of the merger of three smaller Lutheran synods: The Lutheran Church in America (LCA), the American Lutheran Church (ALC), and the Association of Evangelical Lutheran Churches (AELC).

Vital Statistics

The ELCA has 4.8 million members. The ELCA is head-quartered in suburban Chicago. Sources: www.elca.org.

Source of Doctrine

Lutheran church bodies base doctrine on the Scriptures and the Lutheran Confessions. Some church bodies, notably the ELCA, have adopted doctrines from the church bodies they have joined with in fellowship.

Role of Christ/Way of Salvation

Salvation is a free gift given by grace through faith in Christ Jesus. While this teaching remains strong in the Wisconsin Evangelical Lutheran Synod and many of the independent Lutheran churches, the ELCA has joined with other church bodies in recent years and softened its position.

Sacraments

Baptism bestows forgiveness, rescue from death and the devil, and the gift of faith to eternal salvation. In Holy Communion, the participant receives the true body and blood of Christ for forgiveness and strengthening of faith.

Lutheran Response

While we may share the name *Lutheran*, there are considerable differences in doctrine and practice—especially concerning fellowship with other church bodies and the ordination of women.

One Christ, Many Creeds © 2008 Concordia Publishing House. Permission granted to purchaser to reproduce this page for use in educational settings. All other rights reserved.

Church Body

Pentecostal Church

(Assemblies of God USA/ United Pentecostal Church International)

History

The Pentecostal churches trace their history back to the spiritual revivals that took place across the United States in the late 1800s. The modern Pentecostal revival found its beginnings in a prayer meeting held at Bethel College in Topeka on January 1, 1901. By 1914, the Assemblies of God began working together, formulating their "Statement of Fundamental Truths" by 1916.

A sermon on Acts 2:38 was preached by R. E. McAlister in 1913 in which he emphasized that God is known only in the person of Jesus Christ. This oneness theology led to the split between Pentecostals and, ultimately, to the founding of the United Pentecostal Church International in 1945.

Vital Statistics

The Assemblies of God USA lists its membership at 1.6 million. The United Pentecostal Church International lists 600,000 members. The Assemblies of God USA has its headquarters in Springfield, Missouri. The United Pentecostal Church International home office is in suburban St. Louis, Missouri. Sources: www.ag.org; www.upci.org.

Source of Doctrine

Pentecostal churches recognize God's Word found in the Bible as their only source for doctrine. Each individual church body has its own series of statements concerning core beliefs of their particular denomination. For example, the Assemblies of God recognizes the doctrine of the Trinity, while the United Pentecostal Church does not.

Role of Christ/Way of Salvation

According to the Assemblies of God Web site, "Man's only hope of redemption is through the shed blood of Jesus Christ the Son of God. Salvation is received through repentance toward God and faith toward the Lord Jesus Christ. By the washing of regeneration and renewing of the Holy Ghost, being justified by grace through faith, man becomes an heir of God, according to the hope of eternal life." The burden remains on the believer to come to repentance, and the role of the Spirit is emphasized at the expense of Christ.

Sacraments

Baptism is not performed on young children in Pentecostal churches. Immersion is the only correct form of Baptism according to Pentecostal churches. Since they reject the doctrine of the Trinity, the UPCI teaches that Baptism "in the name of Jesus" is the only correct formula for water Baptism.

Pentecostal churches teach that following Baptism all believers should actively desire and seek the "Baptism of the Holy Spirit." This "Spirit Baptism" identifies itself through the individual believer speaking in tongues.

Communion is practiced merely as a remembrance of Christ's sacrifice; the elements include bread and the fruit of the vine (either wine or grape juice).

Lutheran Response

Their focus on Baptism of the Spirit denies Pentecostal believers the full benefit of the Sacraments. Help them see the real benefits of God's Word and promise rather than man's emotional reaction.

One Christ, Many Creeds © 2008 Concordia Publishing House. Permission granted to purchaser to reproduce this page for use in educational settings. All other rights reserved.

BR 516.5 .R68 2008
Rottmann, Erik.
One Christ, many creeds

Churc

Emerging Churches

History

Their individual histories vary, but most Emerging churches build themselves around the preaching and leadership of a pastor with a charismatic personality (e.g., Bill Hybels at Willow Creek and Rick Warren [*Purpose Driven Life*] at Saddleback.)

Vital Statistics

Membership is not recorded in one source. These churches speak more in terms of attendance rather than membership. There is a huge focus on specialized ministries to meet the needs of their membership and visitors. Everything is done on a big scale. Sources: www.willow-creek.org; www.saddleback.com.

Source of Doctrine

Doctrine varies from church to church since there is no standard or national church body.

Role of Christ/Way of Salvation

Emerging churches generally express reformed/evangelical teachings. Salvation is viewed as a gift of God that the individual can choose to accept or reject.

Sacraments

While the Emerging churches may celebrate Baptism and Holy Communion, they generally see them as only symbolic, a way of making a public statement about the individual's belief.

Lutheran Response

It is only possible to respond in a very general way to Emerging churches, since they are constantly being created and changing. A focus on God's work—Christ's suffering and death as objective realities that are central to Christianity is important.

One Christ, Many Creeds © 2008 Concordia Publishing House. Permission granted to purchaser to reproduce this page for use in educational settings. All other rights reserved.